AF334775

Joan Jonas

I Want to Live in the Country (And Other Romances)

Susan Morgan

Afterall Books Editors
Charles Esche and Mark Lewis

One Work Series Editor
Mark Lewis

Contributing Editor
Jan Verwoert

Managing Editor
Caroline Woodley

Other titles in the *One Work* series:

Bas Jan Ader: In Search of the Miraculous
by Jan Verwoert

Hollis Frampton: (nostalgia)
by Rachel Moore

*Ilya Kabakov: The Man Who Flew into Space
from his Apartment*
by Boris Groys

Richard Prince: Untitled (couple)
by Michael Newman

One Work is a unique series of books published by Afterall,
based at Central Saint Martins College of Art and Design
in London. Each book presents a single work of art considered
in detail by a single author. The focus of the series is on
contemporary art and its aim is to provoke debate about
significant moments in art's recent development.

Over the course of more than 100 books, important works
will be presented in a meticulous and generous manner
by writers who believe passionately in the originality and
significance of the works about which they have chosen
to write. Each book contains a comprehensive and detailed
formal description of the work, followed by a critical mapping
of the aesthetic and cultural context in which it was made and
has gone on to shape. The changing presentation and reception
of the work throughout its existence is also discussed and
each writer stakes a claim on the influence 'their' work has
on the making and understanding of other works of art.

The books insist that a single contemporary work of art
(in all of its different manifestations) can, through a unique
and radical aesthetic articulation or invention, affect our
understanding of art in general. More than that, these books
suggest that a single work of art can literally transform,
however modestly, the way we look at and understand the
world. In this sense the *One Work* series, while by no means
exhaustive, will eventually become a veritable library of
works of art that have made a difference.

First published in 2006
by Afterall Books

Afterall
Central Saint Martins
College of Art and Design
University of the Arts London
107—109 Charing Cross Road
London WC2H ODU
www.afterall.org

© Afterall, Central Saint Martins
College of Art and Design, University
of the Arts London, the artists and
the authors.

ISBN Paperback: 1-84638-025-1, 978-1-84638-025-9
ISBN Cloth: 1-84638-026-X, 978-1-84638-026-6

Distribution by The MIT Press, Cambridge,
Massachusetts and London, England
www.mitpress.mit.edu

Art Direction and Typeface Design
A2/SW/HK

Printed and bound by
Die Keure, Belgium

All Joan Jonas images courtesy the artist
and Electronic Arts Intermix, New York

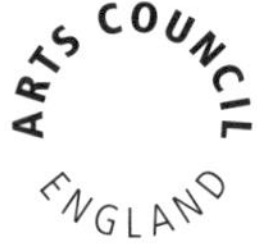

Joan Jonas

I Want to Live in the Country (And Other Romances)

Susan Morgan

I would like to thank Zen Chang, Shirley Irons, Jim Krusoe,
Tom Leeser, Judy Linn, Sarah Kline Morgan, Charles Ruas,
Laurie Spiegel and Pat Steir for their support, good humour
and encyclopedic insights. And, of course, I thank Joan
Jonas for her generous spirit and incomparable originality,
her tireless curiosity and wonderfully compelling vision.

The editors would also like to thank Gaia Alessi, Pablo
Lafuente and Deirdre O'Dwyer.

Susan Morgan is a writer based in Los Angeles, California
and Edinburgh, Scotland. From 1979–1991 she was,
with Thomas Lawson, the co-editor of *Real Life* magazine,
an alternative art publication based in New York. A former
contributing writer for *Interview, Mirabella* and *Elle*, she
is currently a contributing editor at *Metropolitan Home*.
The author of *Martin Munkacsi* (Aperture, 1992) and *Edward
Weston: Portraits* (Aperture, 1995), Morgan is a recipient
of the Center for Creative Photography's Ansel Adams
Research Fellowship.

for tcl, always

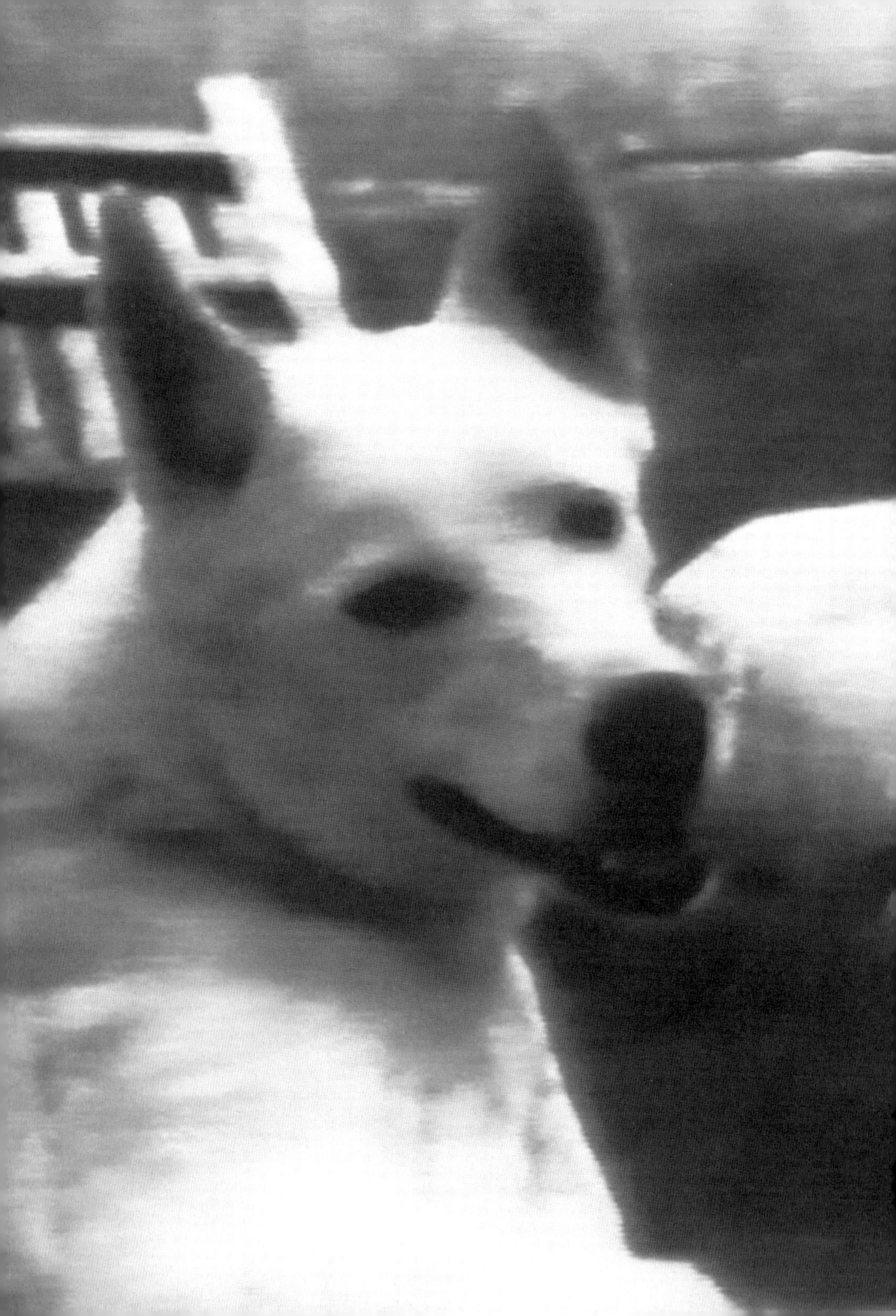

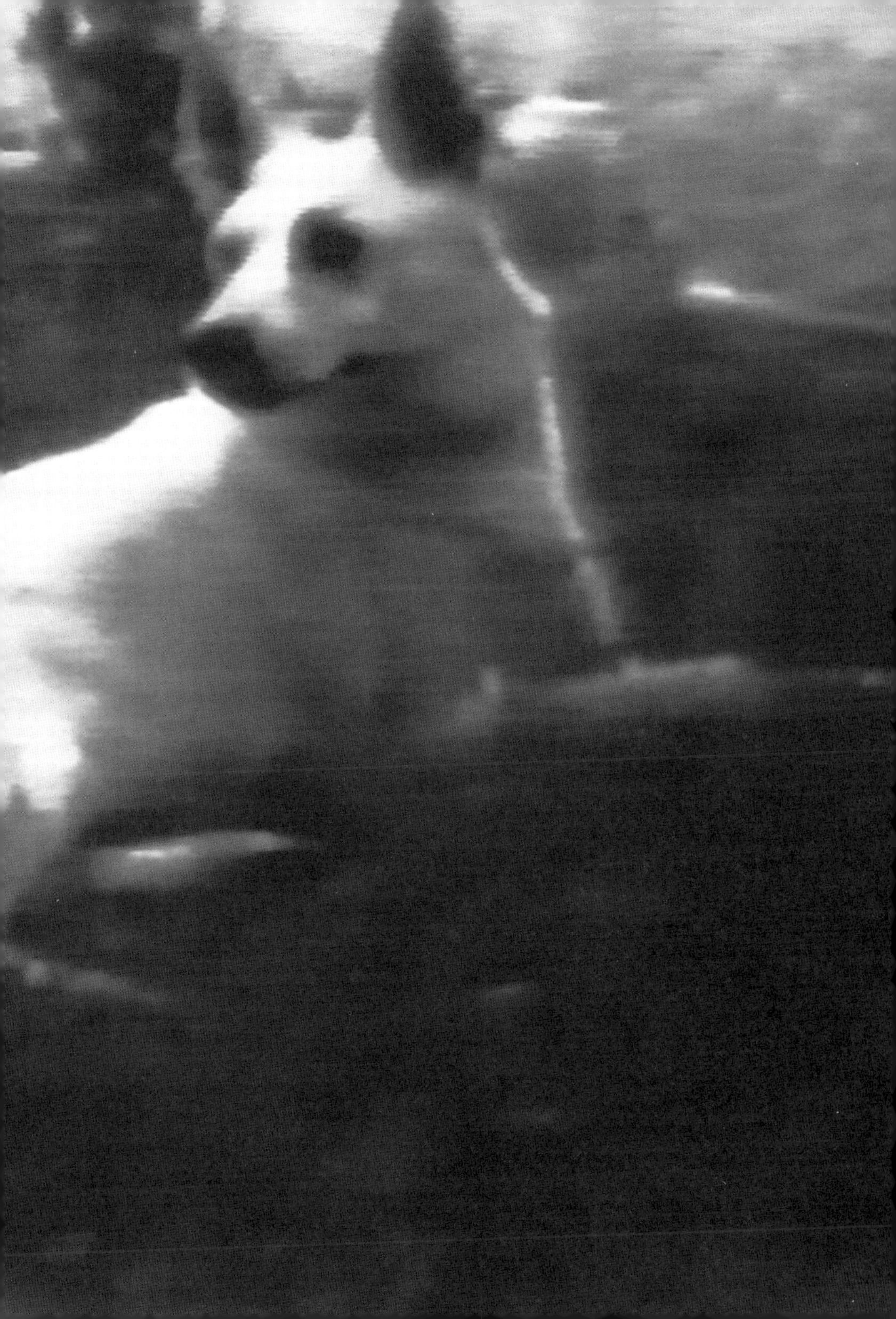

previous page

still from *I Want to Live in
the Country (And Other Romances)*,
video, 1976

*Arise, come hasten, let us abandon the city to merchants,
attorneys, brokers, usurers, tax-gatherers, scriveners,
doctors, perfumers, butchers, cooks, bakers and tailors,
alchemists, painters, mimes, dancers, lute players,
quacks, panderers, thieves, criminals, adulterers, parasites,
foreigners, swindlers and jesters, gluttons who with scent
alert catch the odour of the market place, for whom that
is the only bliss, whose mouths are agape for that alone.*[1]
— Francesco Petrarca (1356)

In 1976 Joan Jonas made a single-channel colour
video called *I Want to Live in the Country (And Other
Romances)*. This 28-minute tape is comprised of 25
vignettes — 13 exterior scenes and 12 interior — that
alternate consistently between two locations: Cape
Breton, Nova Scotia, along the Atlantic coast of rural
Canada; and a windowless room constructed within
a New York City television station's blue screen studio.
On the soundtrack, a woman's voice — low and flinty
— provides an uninflected voiceover narration. Alone,
she reads a random selection of journal entries: cryptic
observations, recalled dreams and everyday concerns.
It's an elliptical narrative, non-linear, open-ended and
purposefully composed from fragments — commonplace
yet arrestingly poetic. No proper names are used and
character descriptions are scarce, nearly nonexistent:
there is a 'man in a red car', but his presence ('wary
but not intrusive') is only mentioned, we never see him.
Although, at times, the text refers to other people —
a grey figure glimpsed in the mist, some friends, a boy
and a group of women — the chronicled situations are
entirely unencumbered by personality, free-floating,

alive in our imaginations. It's an experience akin
to listening to the basic plot of an enduring folktale
or the restrained physical descriptions offered up in
a Jane Austen novel — we are free to picture anyone
we want in these places and situations. Occasionally,
figures do appear in the landscape: two unidentifiable
men cutting down trees and walking away into
the fields, a dark-haired woman frolicking in the
unmown grass with a pair of white dogs. Once, very
fleetingly, framed in a curtained window, we catch
a glance of a woman's upraised arm; her elbow is
bent as if she might be holding binoculars, looking
out to someplace we cannot see. Even in this fairly
wild countryside the sounds and sights of machinery
intrude: passing trucks raise dust clouds on the dirt
road, earth movers dig up a quarry, chain-saws whine
and a motor boat engine rumbles offshore. Mostly,
however, there is the thrumming of wind and waves
and the crackle of spreading fire. In the open air,
we can hear dogs barking, crickets chirping, a scrap
of old-timey Appalachian music playing and the deep
lowing of cows.

Jonas filmed the 13 exterior scenes — filled with
strong sunlight and wild, weather-beaten colour
— during a single Cape Breton summer. She used a
hand-held Super 8 camera and the footage meanders,
generously sweeping over land and sea, capturing a
panorama of falling trees, waves crashing on rocks,
gusts of smoke and tall grasses thrashing in the wind.
The natural world is wide and vibrant and Jonas
fills the screen with it.

In *I Want to Live in the Country (And Other Romances)*
each one of the 12 interior vignettes is presented as
a tightly constructed *mise-en-scène*, a manipulated
still life, a little theatre of the mind. The semi-abstract
set suggests an artist's urban studio; enclosed, well-
considered and fitted out with a changing array of
objects, practical and archetypal: a blackboard, several
wooden chairs, an architectural column, a large sheet
of paper rolled up into a cone, a mirror and a globe of
the world. In describing her work, Jonas has remarked:
'I always thought that the activity of putting one object
next to another was like making a visual poem.'[2]

All of the interior vignettes, staged and improvised,
were shot on video, using three cameras in fixed
positions focused on the set: two cameras were directed
at the set-up while the third was trained on a monitor
that could pick up images from either of the first
two. In this way, the videotaped images were able
to jump around the room and be juggled in multiple
combinations. There is a video monitor that appears
on the screen during the interior segments; keyed in
electronically, it is posted permanently in the lower
right-hand corner of the screen, a frame within a
frame like an animated snapshot tucked into the bigger
picture. During the interior segments, the screen is
divided up and the setting claustrophobic — a static
counterpoint to the rapturous Super 8 footage of the
windswept countryside.

In the opening sequence of *I Want to Live in the Country
(And Other Romances)*, the camera pans slowly across the

landscape, a smudged pastel-coloured view of open
fields leading down to the ocean, an unpaved road,
a profusion of wild hedges and pine trees and a single
house. As the camera ambles leisurely from left to right,
it tracks a rather slow-moving getaway: a wide-bed
pickup truck heads pokily up a small hill and then
disappears from view. The camera then swoops right
to left and back again. Each time, the view — blurred
and lovely as a watercolour wash of a pastoral scene
— changes ever so slightly: the camera pulls back,
revealing a barn, another house, the empty stretch
of road. The first house, glimpsed now in the distance,
seems smaller and smaller. No one appears in the frame
and there is no dialogue or music, only a muffled steady
roar, rhythmic as the changing tide.

The scene then cuts abruptly, radically, to the blue
screen television studio: an illuminated box stage,
a bright blue square sharply outlined in red. It's a
brisk slap to the eye, snapping the viewer from the
soft colours and languorous mood of the rural idyll.
The screen is transformed into a framed picture of the
artificially constructed interior with its somewhat
vertiginous arrangement of actual objects and projected
images. The background sound fades out slowly. Perhaps
there is the drone of cicadas. The voiceover begins. It is
Jonas's voice — hesitant, deliberate and undramatic —
reading: 'There is a room. A big room. With a steeply
pitched roof. Like an attic. It is blue.' Although the
space that appears on the screen is blue, the scene doesn't
necessarily illustrate the text. The objects in the room
— a blackboard, an architectural column — are

rearranged by unseen forces, appearing and disappearing
in the blink of an eye.

In eight of the interior vignettes, a woman (actress
Ellen McElduff) appears. Dressed simply in a full white
cotton skirt and a short-sleeved white cotton blouse
neatly tapered at the waist, she is confined to the studio
and her image is always cropped, often headless. We
never really see her face, only her movements, the blur
of her features and obscuring toss of her hair as she
turns away from the camera. Nevertheless, she takes
centre stage and holds her place there. The austere
interior comes to life with her isolated, rhythmic and
quotidian actions: she sets the globe rapidly spinning,
or plays a sort of antic solo version of musical chairs,
sashaying like a high-spirited square dancer. With
broad graceful strokes, she draws a series of white chalk
arcs — pictographs of hills or rainbows — on the blackboard. 'There is always a woman in my work,' Jonas
has said. 'And her role is questioned.'[3]

In another interior sequence, however, the woman
deftly concedes her place centre stage, and a classical
statue of a black horse looms into view. An immobile
artefact, with its handsome, imperious head and
great, sloping back, the horse is a rare beauty with
unquestionable theatrical presence. Edited with quick
cuts, no dissolves or fades, the horse appears as other
objects in the room — the globe and architectural
column — are continuously shuffled. Suddenly, the
looming horse seems to disappear only to pop up again
in the background, looking small as a knick-knack on

its tidy base. 'The spaces I made were intellectual, historical and stuffed with historical references carrying the past,' the voiceover intones. 'Stifling me in the hot blue cellar.' The voice is candid, calm and unsentimental; the text seems to present neither a plea nor a complaint. In the background there is the buzz of a chain-saw and the refrain of the Appalachian tune breaking down into a yodel.

Exterior: As the yodeling fades out, the buzz of the chain-saw grows louder and the camera moves in to a close-up shot with greenery filling the screen, thatched with pine branches. A man's arm reaches out from the right of the screen and tips over a freshly cut tree. Everything appears in slight slow motion: pine boughs tumble, wood chips fly like sparks into the air and the man lopes away from the camera in long, easy strides. As the buzzing dims, the voiceover says:

The air was totally still. With the smoke rising over the trees, the sun orange through the flames, each dry pine burned like an inferno. Throwing off an intense bright heat. Lucky there was no wind. A fire's speed is seldom seen in these parts.

As the scenes alternate sharply back and forth between the studio and the landscape, the voiceover contributes a sense of watchfulness, daily pleasure and a teetering equilibrium. Travelling between places and ideas, the artist remains a perpetual observer, distanced but tinged with longing. In the final sequences, a pale, whirling globe cuts to a field of yellow wildflowers stirring in the breeze against a brilliant, cloudless sky.

The voiceover states plainly:

*I am an immigrant here. Carrying in my heart a myth
as support from another place where I do not wish to return.
From this land I am occupying. And I fell in love the
first morning.*

I Want to Live in the Country (And Other Romances) was
produced during a particularly vibrant moment in
the continuing cycle of twentieth-century avant-garde
performance and the burgeoning history of video art.
It's dizzying now to encounter a timeline charting
the development of video technology and new media
art from the 1960s through the 70s: during these two
decades, video evolved from an unknown quantity into
a cultural contender.[4]

I Want to Live in the Country (And Other Romances)
was made in 1976 for broadcast viewing, while
Jonas was an artist-in-residence with the Television
Laboratory programme at WNET/Channel 13 in New
York City. Still a flagship station of the National Public
Broad-casting Service, Channel 13 was founded in 1952
as the National Educational Television channel; in 1972
WNET/Channel 13, with funding from the Rockefeller
Foundation and New York State Council on the Arts's
newly developed video grants, sponsored the TV Lab.
Under the directorship of David Loxton, the programme
opened the station's state-of-the-art broadcast video
technology to independent artists, painters and choreog-
raphers. Working with the TV Lab's engineers and
equipment, resident artists — including Peter Campus,

Hermine Freed, Kit Fitzgerald and John Sanborn and
Woody and Steina Vasulka — were invited to create
new and experimental videotapes. During this period
potential support and exhibition opportunities for
new video appeared like some sort of counter-cultural
Camelot: for one brief moment, there was a hint that
alternative media practice and a televisual art might
find financing and a wider audience. At one time
in 1975, the Television Lab — with its experimental
videos made by artists — was said to be responsible
for more than 75 percent of the station's programming.
In 1984, the residency programme ended.[5]

When Jonas made *I Want to Live in the Country (And
Other Romances)*, it was the first time she had worked
in colour and with language. At the television station,
shooting the interiors, Jonas utilised a special effect,
the blue screen studio, also for the first time. Blue
screen, or chroma key process, is a visual effect developed
in the 1950s that makes it possible to combine two
pieces of footage in a single shot; it allows, for example,
a suited-up TV weatherman to stand in front of a blank
screen and conjure a barrage of changing images —
hurricane flood watches or a light dusting of snow that
sweep over the dizzily reconfiguring map. In making
one of these composite images, a subject is first photographed against the blue screen, which is an evenly
lit, bright, monochromatic background; that blue screen
shot is then re-photographed through a blue filter;
finally, the original background is removed and replaced
with a different image or scene. As Arthur Widnmer,
the inventor of the blue screen process, once explained:

If you want to have a couple sitting at a cafe in Paris you could send the couple to Paris and hire a crew and get all the lights and stop the traffic and shoot it, but that would be very expensive. Instead, you get a little mock-up on the stage of the table and chairs and set the couple there and shoot them against the blue screen in the background.[6]

While shooting the video sequences Jonas worked without a script; she placed objects in the blue screen studio and improvised movement. The artist's studio set that appears in *I Want to Live in the Country (And Other Romances)* has been compared to a de Chirico painting, an imagined, mysterious space built from odd perspectives and classical motifs.[7] Improvising with objects, transformations occur: a large sheet of drawing paper is rolled up into a cone and becomes a megaphone, then a pirate's spyglass, then a gondolier's oar; a chalk circle drawing of the sun is sliced with one curved line and turns into a crescent moon. In the lower right-hand corner of the screen black-and-white videos play on the spectral monitor, a shadowy mirror reflecting the inexplicable activities in the unreal room. Curiously, this ephemeral arrangement — of props, live performance, drawings and concurrently playing videotapes — in an imagined space directly anticipates the major installations that Jonas started to show nearly twenty years later. When invited to do a retrospective exhibition at the Stedelijk Museum in Amsterdam in 1994, she decided to create gallery installations incorporating the stage sets and objects she had made for her performances, showing them

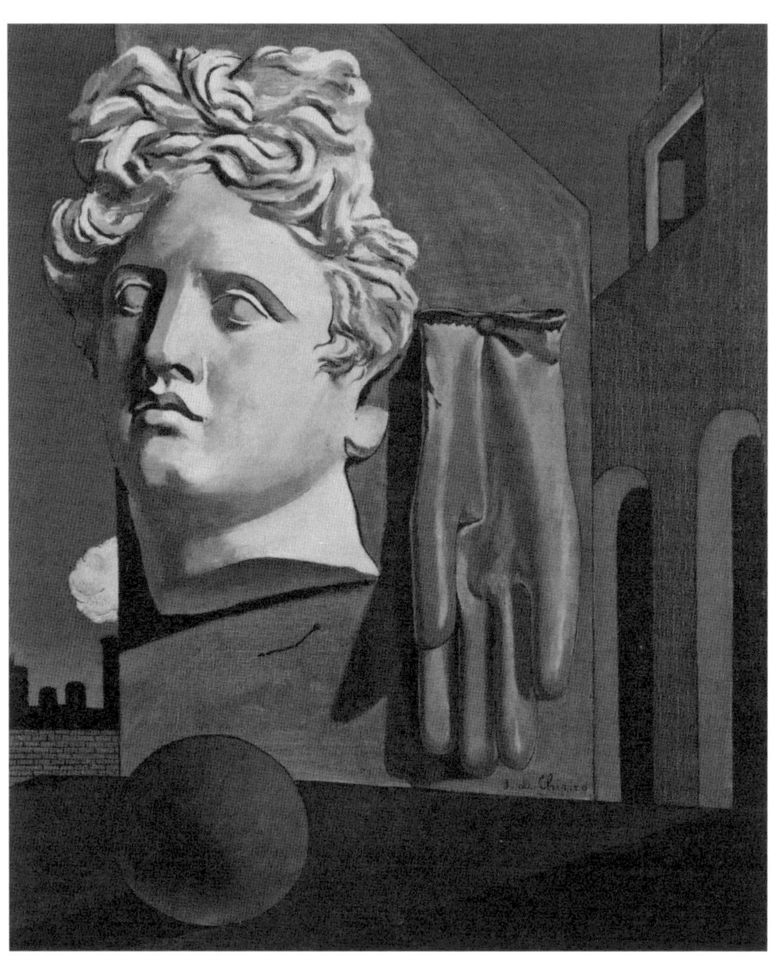

together with videos and newly generated live versions
of earlier performance works.

In *I Want to Live in the Country (And Other Romances)*
the objects in the blue screen studio rearrange themselves in fluid repetition like a constructivist's jittery
slide show of tilting planes and geometric forms.
The voice-over is just above a murmur, certain but
elusive: 'The windows of the house are small. High.'
She pauses. 'So that when you sit, all you see is sky.'
Like a de Chirico painting, where the recognisable
is sited confidently alongside the unknown, the effect
is destabilising, resonant and enigmatic.

Jonas has described video as alchemical and transformative. 'I think of myself as a kind of medium for
information to pass through,' she has said, articulating
an essential aspect of her working methods.[8] 'Like other
artists in the early twentieth century I was thinking
of the three-ringed circus. It's really about me wanting
to say certain things. And I wanted to create a magic
show.'[9] For Jonas, video — with its virtuosic capacity
for reflection, illusion, repetition, manipulation,
simultaneity and revisions — extended the boundaries
of performance and expanded the story-telling language
of forms that is essential to her work. As a teenager
in the 1950s, Jonas watched TV comedies, fresh shows
that toyed with visual reality, incongruous pairings of
image and sound, illusions and intimate performance.[10]
George Burns and Gracie Allen — an endearing, off-
kilter marriage of comic deadpan and madcap reasoning
— transitioned successfully from vaudeville stage to

radio and television. When their show premiered in
1950 a living-room set was surrounded by a proscenium
arch: ordinary domestic life was self-consciously
framed in theatrical artifice. Throughout the show,
Burns would step out of a scene, abandon his own
domestic high-jinks and break the theatrical fourth
wall. Pausing to smoke a cigar and make remarks,
Burns conversed directly with the audience at home.
From 1952 – 1956, Ernie Kovacs — a fantastically
unorthodox comedian — created and starred in a
series of television shows: *Ernie in Kovacsland*, *Kovacs
Unlimited* and simply *The Ernie Kovacs Show*. 'I'd like to
thank you all for inviting me into your living rooms,'
Kovacs would announce looking out from the television.
'It's just a shame you didn't straighten up a little.'
Kovacs was the undisputed master of camera-conscious
comedy. He used video trickery to make candle flames
float in the air and pilots fly without planes. Kovacs
would reverse a scene like a photographic negative
or flip the broadcast image suddenly upside down.
On screen Kovacs spoke to the camera crew and wandered
down the studio corridors. He built a set on a slant —
a table and chairs, pictures hanging on the walls —
and filmed it with a camera set at the exact same angle,
squaring the scene and making it appear level. When
a hapless character sits down at the table, every object
he places on the tabletop inexplicably rolls away.[11]
Kovacs's television imagery was original and hallucinatory. On *I Love Lucy*, Ethel and Lucy's lives remained
more enclosed within the confines of the television
set: they just got gussied up and wanted to be in
Ricky's show.

In Jonas's childhood the everyday and the magical
were, at times, uniquely interwoven: her stepfather
was an amateur magician. She grew up with magic
shows and 1940s Broadway musicals, Rodgers and
Hammerstein's *Carousel* and *Oklahoma*, romantic
plots full of bright tunes and dances that were laced
with a dark undercurrent of brooding soliloquies and
introspective dream ballets. 'I wanted to make a magic
show,' Jonas has stated. 'But I like to reveal the way
the illusions are made.'[12] As a student, she had never
taken any part in theatre. She has described her shyness
as extreme: 'I couldn't even speak to people. Yvonne
Rainer and I realised we were both shy but we both
loved to perform.'[13] Performing was transformative:
mirrors, masks and video monitors could be used to
generate an entirely separate identity — one that was
other, distanced and public.

In her contribution to *Video Art*, a landmark anthology
published in 1976, Jonas writes:

*Video is a device extending the boundaries of my interior
dialogue to include the audience. The perception is of a
double reality: me as image and as performer. I think of
the work in terms of imagist poetry; disparate elements
juxtaposed... alchemy.*[14]

Often considered alongside the contemporaneous work
of Peter Campus and Vito Acconci, Jonas's earliest videotapes (from 1968–72) are not generally described in
terms of the alchemical power of televisual illusion.
Rather, they are discussed in terms of an analytical

and self-reflective exploration of the video medium and the basic relation of body/camera/monitor: acted out alone, in the isolated environment of a studio or gallery space, an artist treats the video monitor as an ongoing mirror. When the video camera is turned to look directly into the monitor, the information flows in a continuous loop: this video feedback produces a complex spatial and temporal dynamic, an infinite mirroring effect. Shooting with video Jonas was able to watch herself improvising and developing content for her performances and tapes. Alternatively, while collaborating with a camera person before an audience, Jonas's live performances scrutinised the discrepancy between the camera's viewpoint and the spectator's; in real time, live action and closed circuit television images appeared together, simultaneous yet slightly out of sync, contrasting and disrupting one another.

In 1972 Jonas made *Organic Honey's Visual Telepathy* (black-and-white, 23min); it's a work that brings together video's relentless knack for disruption and repetition while exploring its fascinating capacity to produce televisual illusions. Presented as a live performance incorporating a single-channel video, it starred Jonas as Organic Honey, a masked seductress performing for the glowing world within the television monitor. Organic Honey — whose name had been handily borrowed from the label on a jar in Jonas's kitchen — developed over a period of two years. Like one of the poet Fernando Pessoa's many heteronyms, Organic Honey was a fully invented persona, a separate, flamboyant entity and creator of her own world.[15]

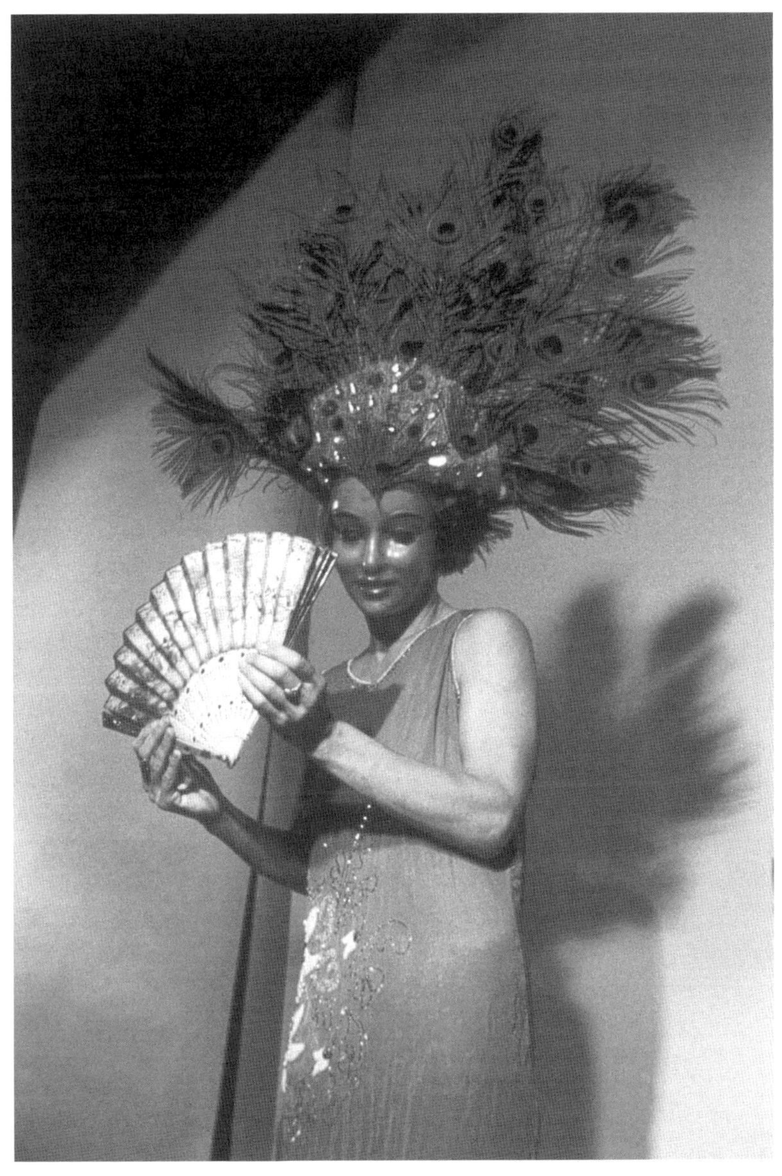

Organic Honey wore antique dresses and kimonos found
at a Los Angeles flea market, and a doll's face mask
bought from a store specialising in erotica. She was
a temptress, a fascinated narcissist at play with her
own image. Shot by photographer Roberta Neiman,
the recorded video version of *Organic Honey's Visual
Telepathy* (which Jonas liked to call 'a film') was
shown on WNET/Channel 13 as part of its ambitious
programming goal to present experimental work to
regular television viewers.

For a visual artist in the twentieth century, the
technology of television opened up an entirely new bag
of tricks. 'Every move was for the monitor,' Jonas has
recalled. 'I tried to climb into the box, attempting to
turn the illusion of flatness to one of depth.'[16] Among
the many tricks on offer, the phenomenon of live video
feedback was a particularly giddy ruse. *Organic Honey's
Vertical Roll* (1972, black-and-white, 20min) was shot off
of a video monitor, the image made to jump incessantly
as two out-of-sync frequencies produced the unstable
effect known as 'vertical roll'. The effect was very
familiar to 1950s television viewers who were
regularly catapulted from their sofas to 'adjust the
picture'. In *Vertical Roll*, Jonas plays electronic jump
rope, hopping over the black bar that scrolls incessantly
up the screen and crashes down with a terrible bang.
On-screen, her hands appear to clap as the rolling effect
pushes the two separate images together. In *Good Night
Good Morning* (1976, black-and-white, 11min), which she
shot in her New York loft and Cape Breton house, Jonas
recorded herself, over the period of a week, as she was

about to go to bed and when she'd just woken up.
Twice each day she looks straight into the camera:
'Good Morning,' she says first, and later, just before
going to sleep, 'Good Night.' Jonas shot the tape with
a camera lying on its side, a pillow-talk perspective;
the completed video is shown upright, played on
a vertical monitor. Climbing in and out and around
the television set, Jonas discovered a playful territory
capable of encompassing great ideas.

In all of the studio sequences in *I Want to Live in the
Country (And Other Romances)*, there is an unmoving
woman (Jonas) posed in semi-profile. She is an
electronic presence, still as a portrait bust with
upswept hair and a slender alabaster neck, steadfastly
positioned in the lower left-hand corner of the screen.
We cannot see her face as she looks straight ahead,
a lonely, riveted audience member gazing into the
inconstant, fabricated space. We can only imagine that
she is looking. Her position never changes; she is a fixed
figure like a paper doll in the front row of a Victorian
toy theatre, or one of those wise-cracking robot silhou-
ettes who heckled schlock movies on *Mystery Science
Theatre 3000*, the 1990s cult television show. In *I Want
to Live in the Country (And Other Romances)* Jonas appears
only as this silent audience member trapped in the
corner of the screen. As Samuel Beckett once riddled
with Delphic wit: 'I am both the observer and the object
that I observe. Which of the two is the real "I"?'[17]

Video provided Jonas with a crucible in which her
free-ranging knowledge could be ingeniously realised

in a *sui generis* form. In a conversation recorded for the catalogue accompanying her 2003 exhibition at the Queens Museum of Art in New York, Jonas explained:

I wasn't trained in video art or performance. Nobody was, in the early 1960s. There was nothing to be trained in because there was no tradition of video or performance; it was totally new territory. There were artists working in dance and there were Happenings, but it wasn't a school. When contemporary American artists first started going to Europe, I remember Philip Glass saying, 'the Europeans think we're primitives'. That was the advantage of being American; we were fresh and the language was fresh.[18]

In 1970, while traveling in Japan, Jonas bought a Sony Portapak — one of the first popular hand held video cameras.[19] As an artist creating cross-disciplinary performance work — combining movement, disparate imagery, sounds and quoted text — Jonas acknowledged that she had a desire to make films: like a filmmaker, time and space were her materials. Although the Portapak — with its low resolution, 3/4inch, black-and-white tape — was unrefined technologically, it was also enticingly portable, inexpensive and miraculously immediate. Video provided a mesmerizing perceptual tool: it was possible to play with time, the simultaneity and the slight distortions of feedback. Articulated gestures framed and recorded on videotape could be cropped, distanced, repeated, manipulated and reconsidered. Working with live feed, video operated in real time and offered the chance to edit on camera: it was ideally suited for improvisation and aleatory events. 'I had

wanted to make films and here was a medium in which
I could make instant sequences of images,' Jonas recalled
in a 1994 interview with Joan Simon. 'I was making
videos, but I was referring to film all the time.'[20]

Originally trained as a sculptor, Jonas later studied
ancient Greek and Chinese art as well as twentieth-
century modernist poetry. When she began to make
performance work in 1968, the influence of film —
as a time-based form, incorporating cuts and edits and
providing a seemingly infinite facility for alterations
and visual recombinations — was already evident.
Jonas had been entranced by the dream-like narratives,
montage effects and ineffable magic captured in early
French and Russian films: Jean Vigo's *L'Atalante* and
its ethereal underwater scene where the young barge
owner is reunited, beneath the Seine, with his lost
bride; the innovative and discordant mix of sound and
images in Dziga Vertov's *Enthusiasm: Donbass Symphony*;
the luxuriant theatrical artifice, gestural authority
and wordless moral tensions of Marcel Carné's *Children
of Paradise*. Jonas wrote in 1983:

*While I was studying art history I looked carefully at the
space of paintings, films and sculpture — how illusions are
created within framed space and how to deal with a real
physical space with depth and distance. When I switched
from sculpture to performance, I just went into a space
and looked at it.*[21]

Jonas has drolly referred to her work as being made in
the stops that occur somewhere along the line between

Conceptual art and theatre. Her sensibility is surprising
and original, balanced unexpectedly between the
compelling precision of imagist poetry and an almost
surrealist proclivity for startling juxtapositions.
The consistent array of objects that she uses — mirrors,
television monitors, masks and folding fans, the
blackboard, even the white dog with one blue eye
— function as archetypes, a dexterous vocabulary of
resonant symbols. Performance, for Jonas, was a way
to combine elements — movement, image and sound
— and produce a complex, layered statement.

As a student of art history Jonas was interested in
the visual record and cultural legacies of early civilisa-
tions. In 1966, while visiting Crete and its spectacular
Bronze Age archeological sites, she attended a wedding
ceremony in the mountains. The ceremony lasted three
days. 'It was a ritual and I was always interested in
folk culture,' she said, 'because it is a part of everyday
life and anybody can be a part of it.'[22] Ritual, with
its vibrant mingling of ancient traditions and everyday
experience, inhabits the inventive ground that Robert
Rauschenberg has so aptly called 'the gap between art
and life'.

In the catalogue for Jonas's retrospective at the Stedelijk
Museum, Richard Serra contributed a wonderful bit of
memoir. In Serra's reminiscence, 'Impromptu February
1968', he writes about Jonas's extraordinary move into
performance, and her discovery of an intricate territory
of double realties, mutable images, transformations and
dislocating perspectives. 'Late one evening I was sitting

on the floor on a mattress in Joan's loft,' Serra begins
his story. Jonas, who is at work on a performance,
asks if he will act as her audience. 'I really did not
know what to expect,' he recalls. The lights are turned
off and Jonas disappears. When she returns, she is
unrecognisable, dressed in a dark, blue hooded silk robe.

*Joan was swaddled in a fetish of cloth, a witch's sacred
bathrobe. A theatrical persona had appeared, a new creation
of sorts was striding towards me with a lighted candle
in a makeshift candle holder. The personality of Joan was
long gone, a fiction. In her place was a magical invocation.*

The hooded figure slowly places the candle and an
ornate tortoiseshell hand mirror on the floor. 'I feel
a bit uneasy,' writes Serra. 'I am losing my distance.'
The hooded figure kneels and grovels, entering into
a private ritual, some spellbinding but enigmatic
act of initiation. Slowly and carefully, she unrolls
a velvet cutlery pouch and removes a sterling silver
serving spoon.

*There is a sober wooden countenance to the hooded figure.
She remains erect, stiff and still, knees bent under her torso,
sitting on her heels, she begins to mechanically tap the spoon
on the floor beside the mirror. This goes on seemingly forever
while her eyes are transfixed on her reflection. Her arm lifts
above the shoulder, the elbow bends and in an instant the
spoon is raised overhead and brought down with full force,
striking the glass and smashing the mirror; with the first
blow — no crisis, the figure remains composed but then the
beating of the spoon upon the mirror takes on an ugly aspect,*

*as it is repeated over and over again until every vestige
is broken down into crystals, into fractured geometries
of pain. This is no surgical operation, this is punishment,
pure and simple. It is as if the mirror has been beaten to
death. There must have been forty or fifty blows administered
to this narcissistic fetish; and as suddenly as it started,
it stopped, the figure exhausted. Joan got up, turned on
the lights, smiled and asked, 'What did you think of the
performance?'*[23]

In 1971 Jonas and Serra collaborated on two short films: *Paul Revere* and *Veil*. The script for *Paul Revere* (16mm, black-and-white, 9min) — a didactic voiceover narration read by Jonas — was taken from anthropologist Ray L. Birdwhistell's 1970 book *Kinesics and Context: Essays on Body Motion Communication*.[24] 'Kinesics' was a term first used by Birdwhistell in 1952; his studies focused on non-verbal communication, how ideas are expressed through posture, gesture, stance and movement — what became commonly known as 'body language'. Jonas, who had participated in dance workshops given by Deborah Hay, Yvonne Rainer and Trisha Brown, shared the dancers' interest in freely improvising with everyday movement and child's play, and rendering the familiar as newly strange. Reading Birdswhitsell, Serra observed that Jonas's performances were structured utilising gestures and body signals, and composed like edited films with visual cuts marking the swift transition from one action to another.[25]

Veil (1971, video, black-and-white, 6min), is based on Kenneth Anger's *Puce Moment* (1949, 35mm, colour,

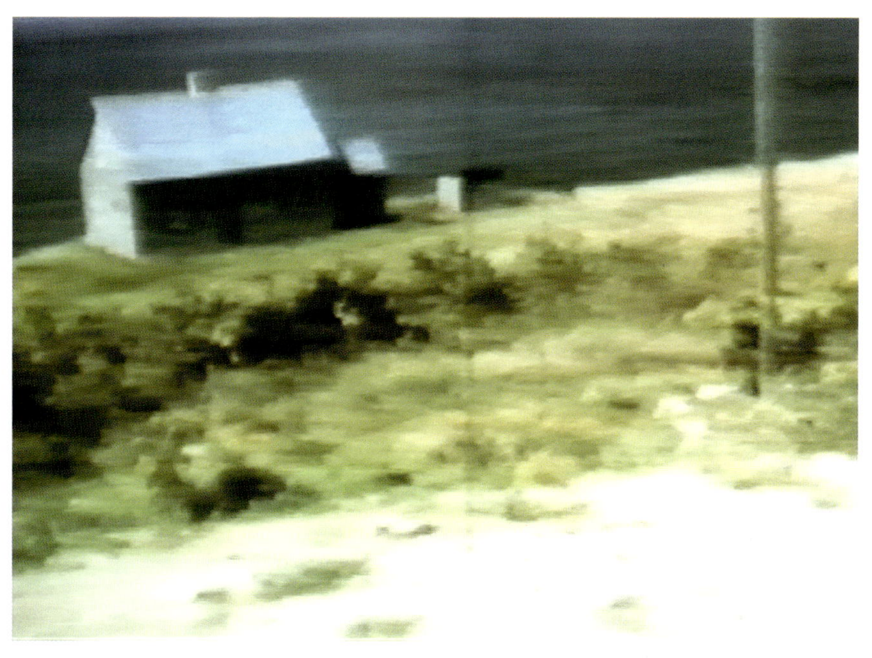

1—34. stills from *I Want to Live in the Country (And Other Romances)*, video, 1976

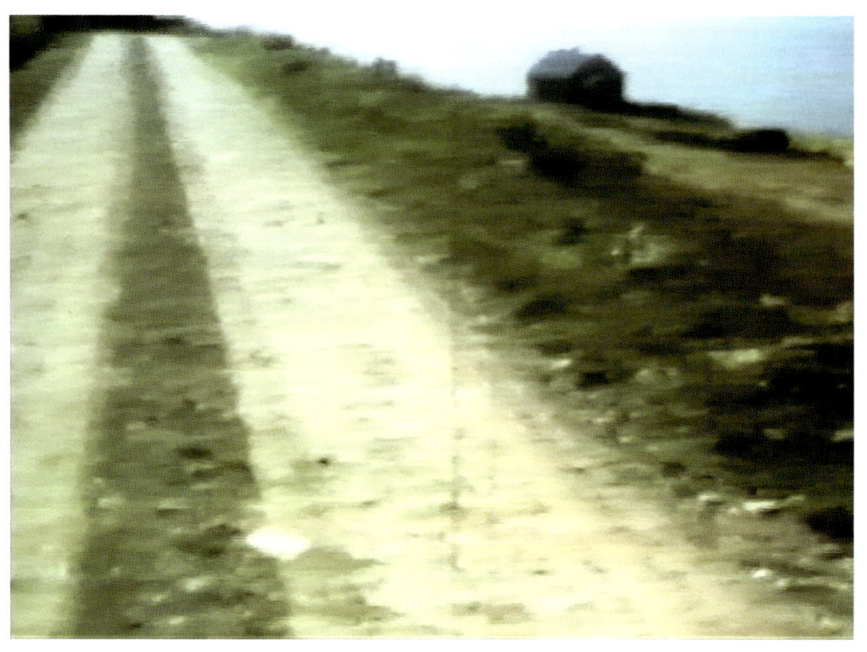

2.

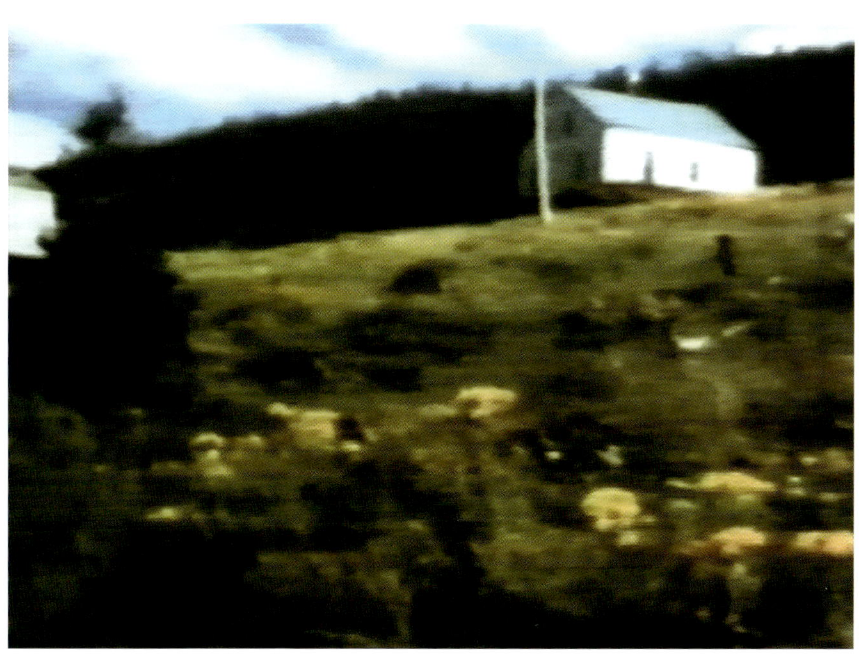

3.

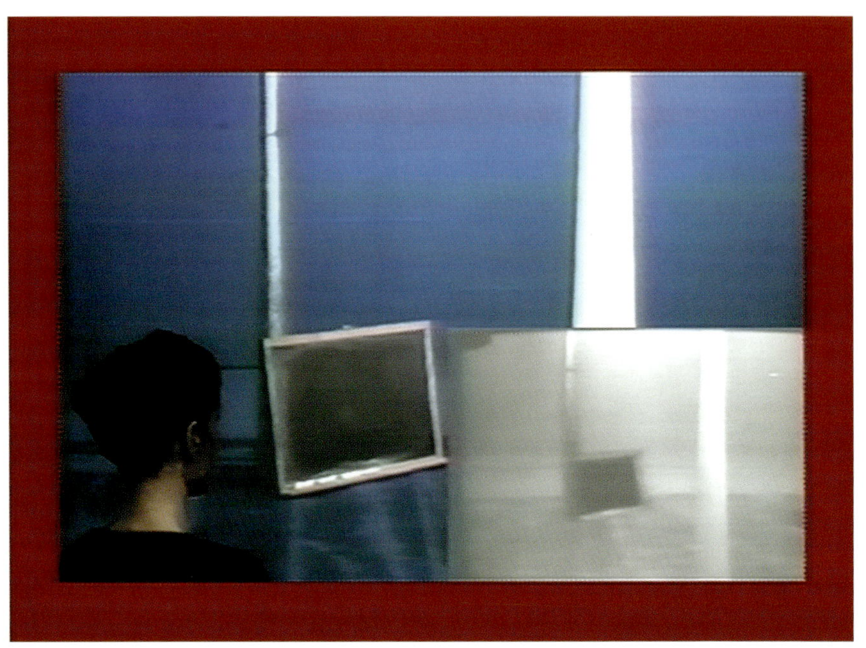

4.

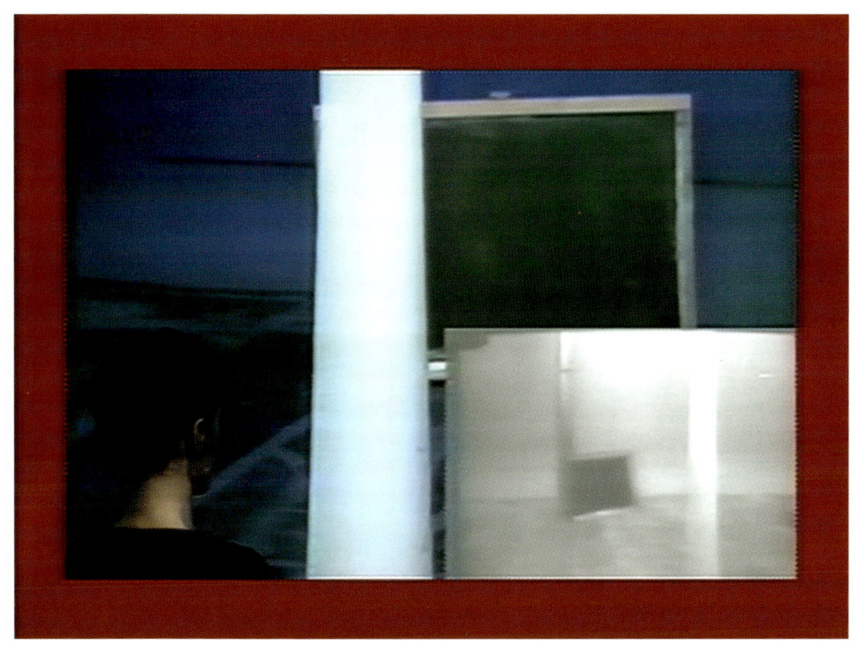

5.

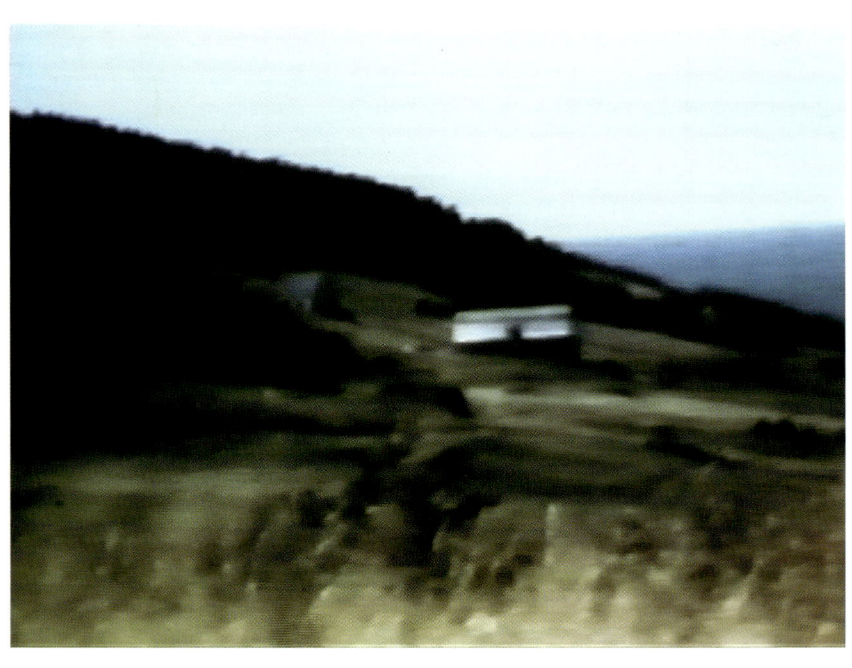

6.

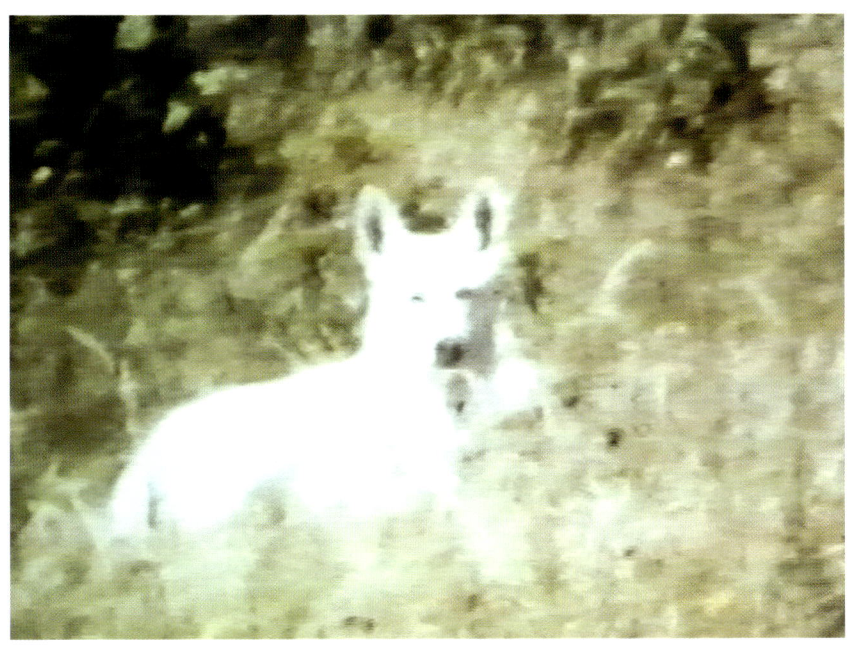

7.

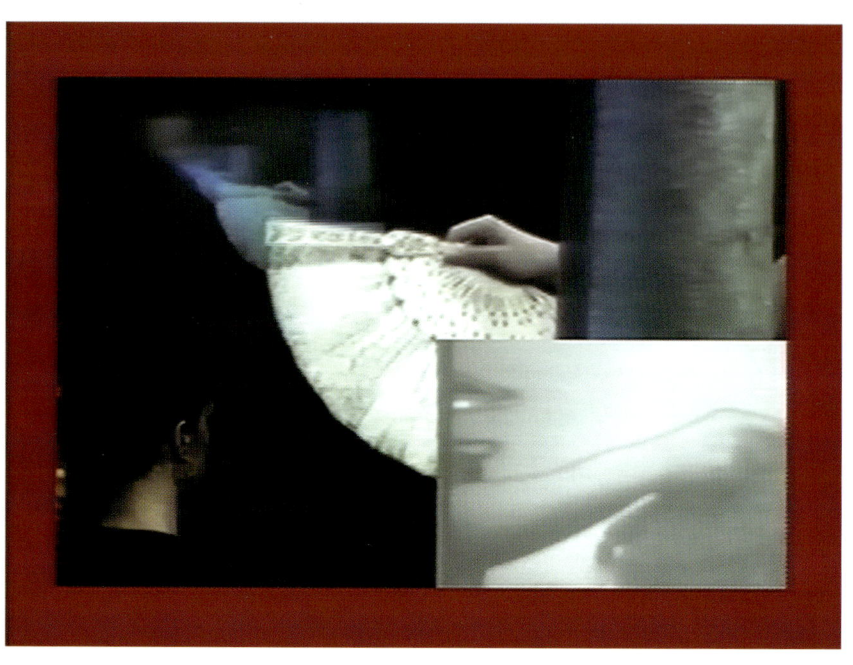

8.

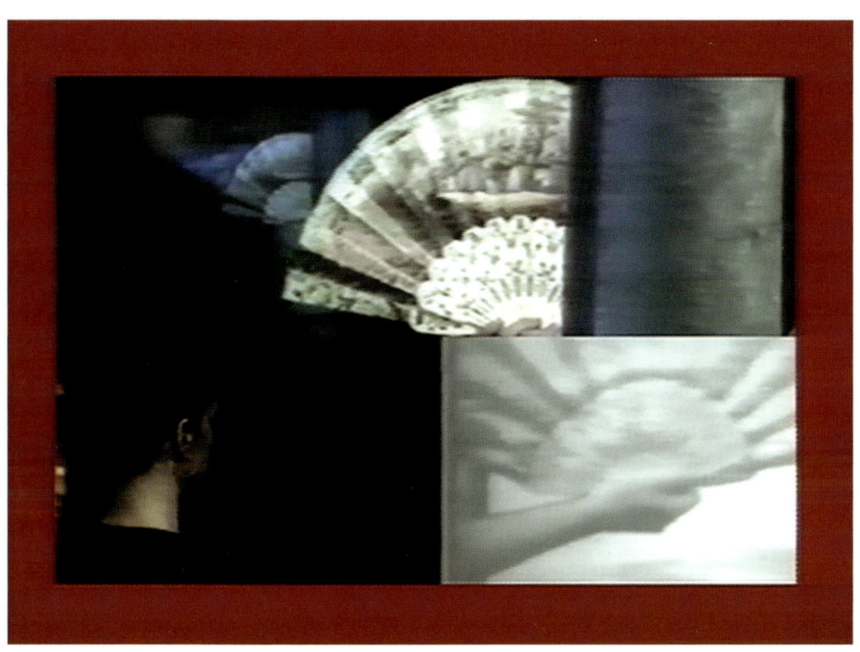

9.

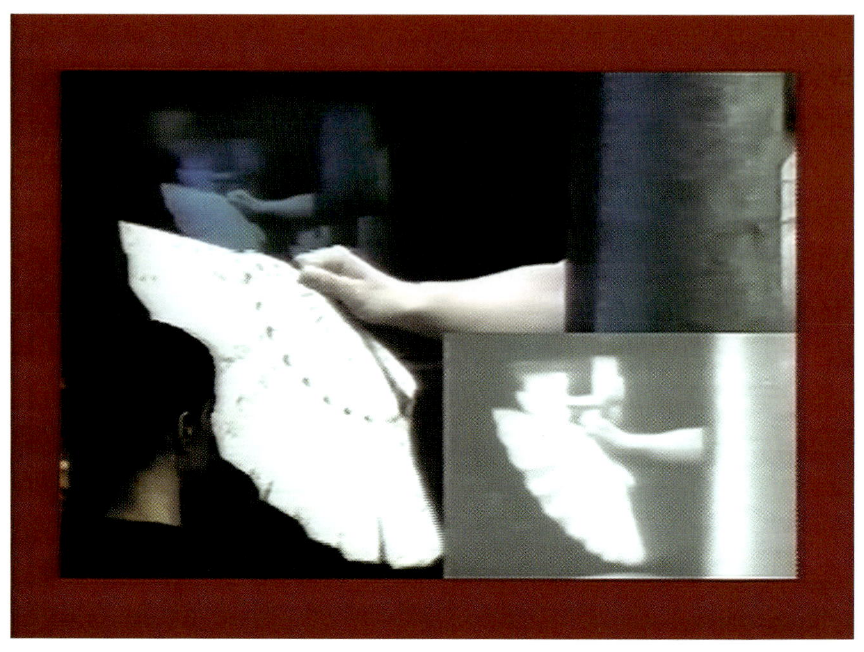

10.

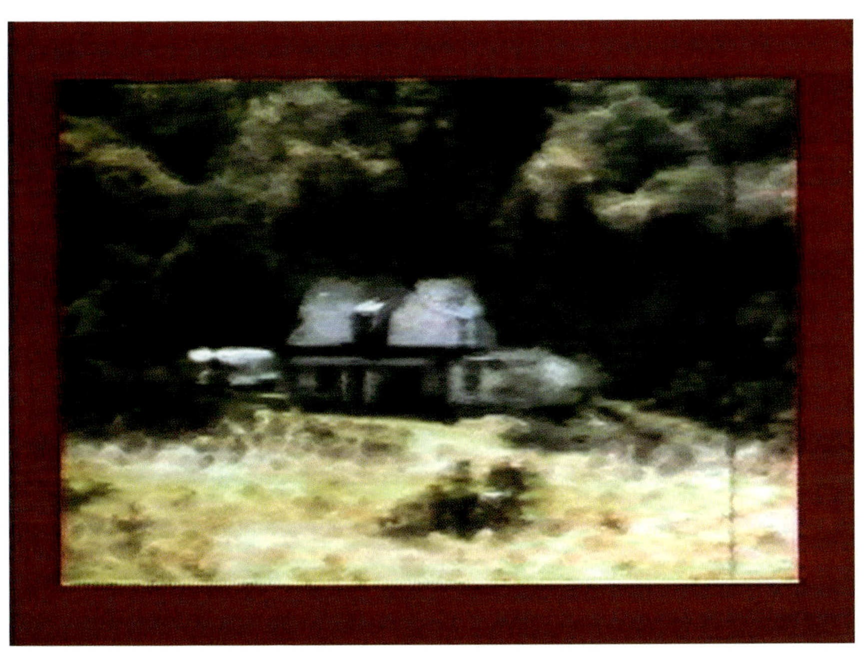

11.

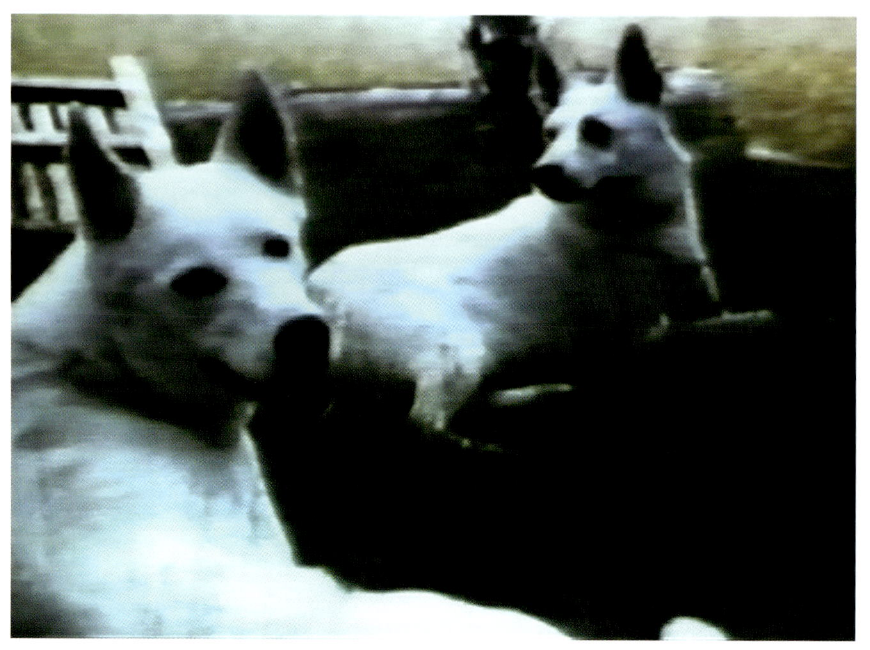

12.

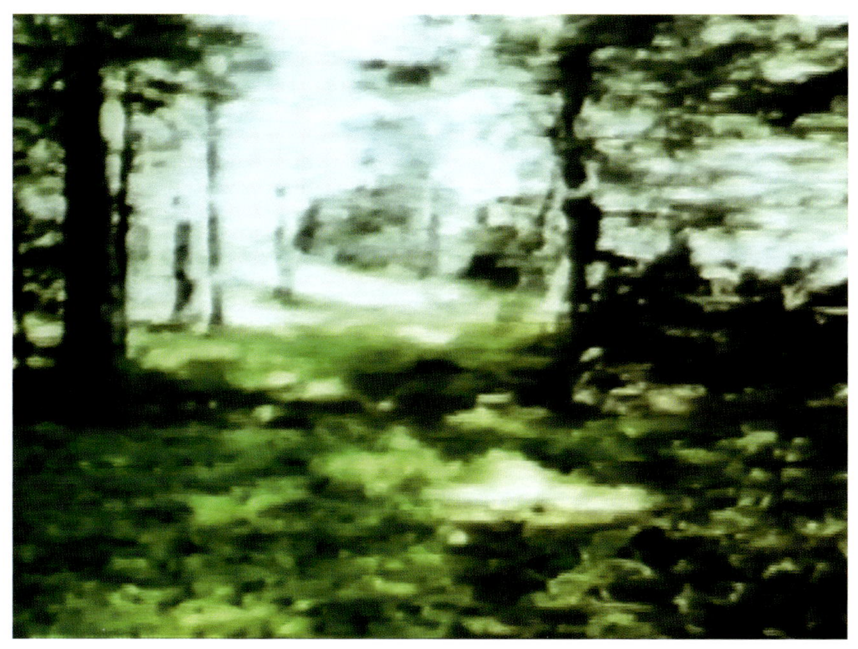

13.

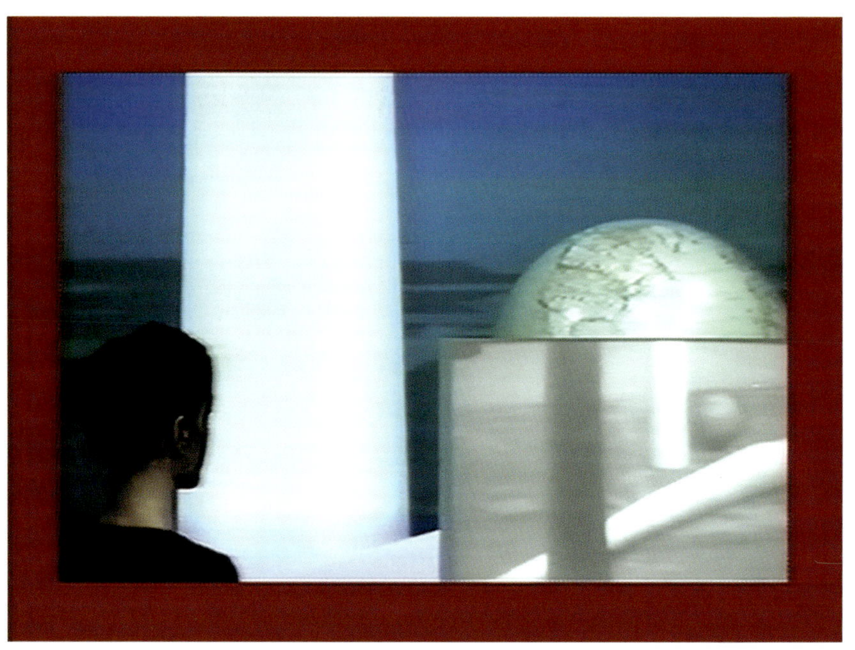

14.

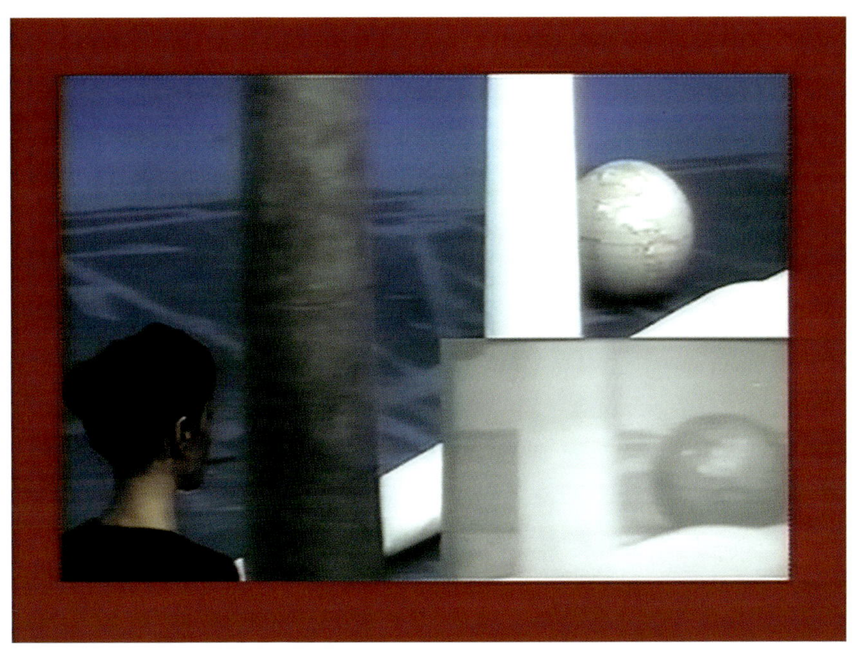

15.

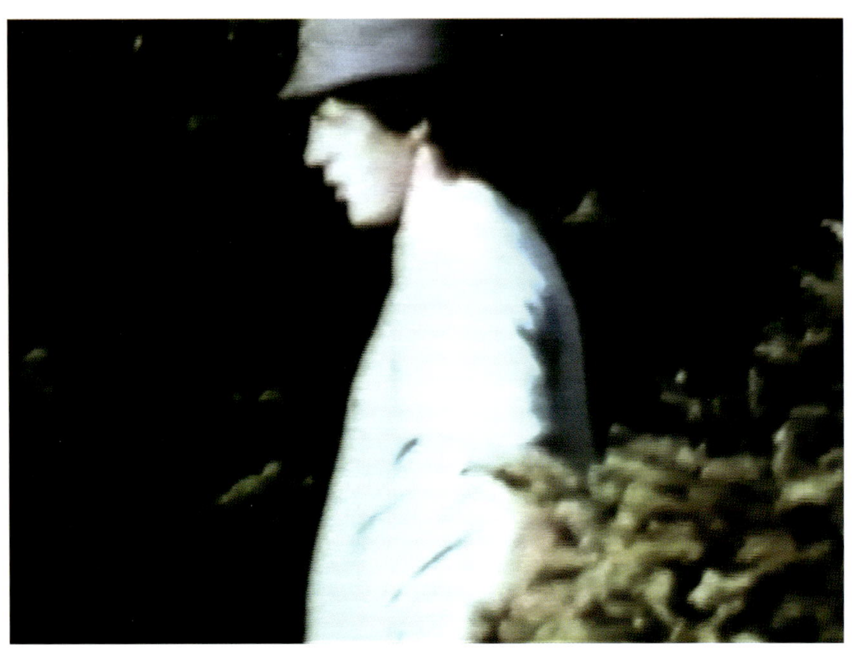

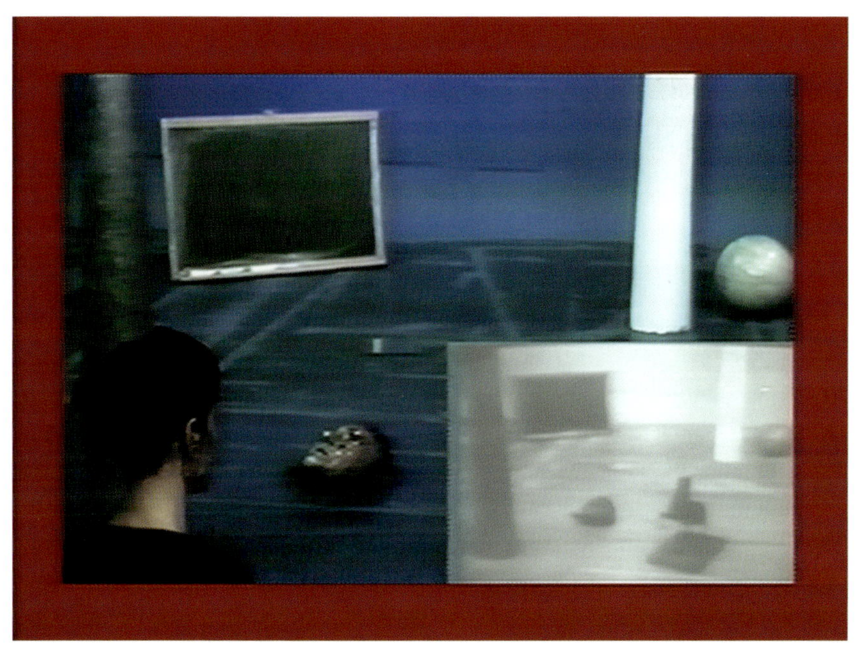

17.

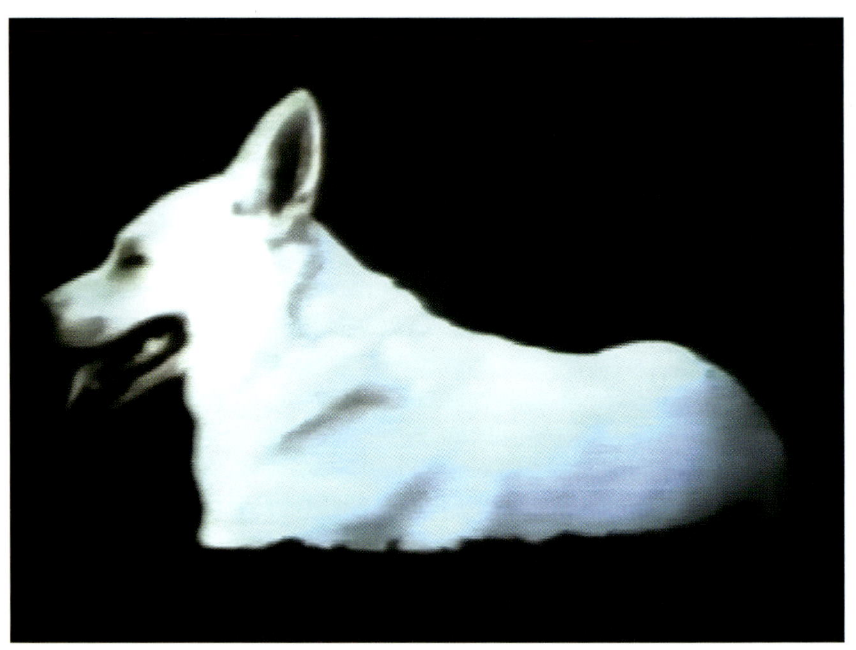

18.

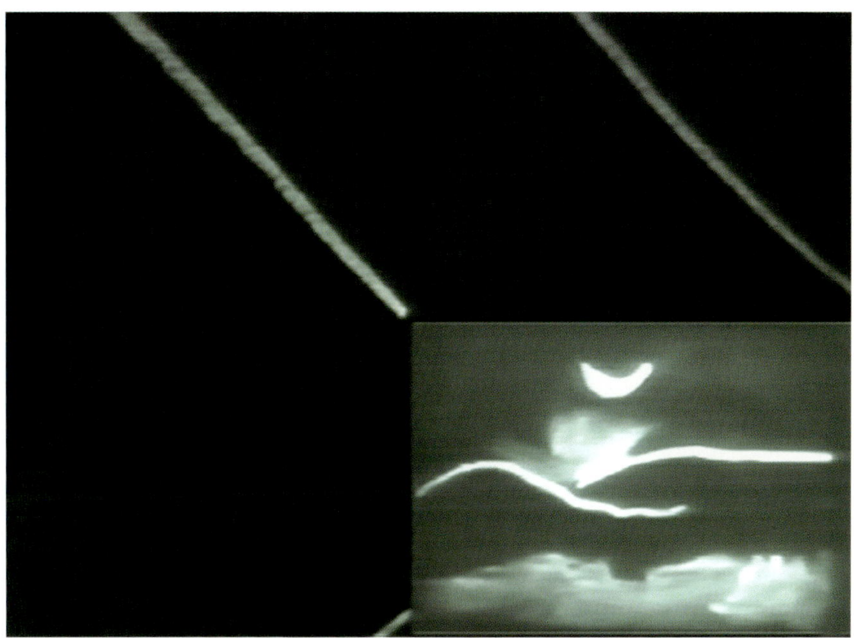

19.

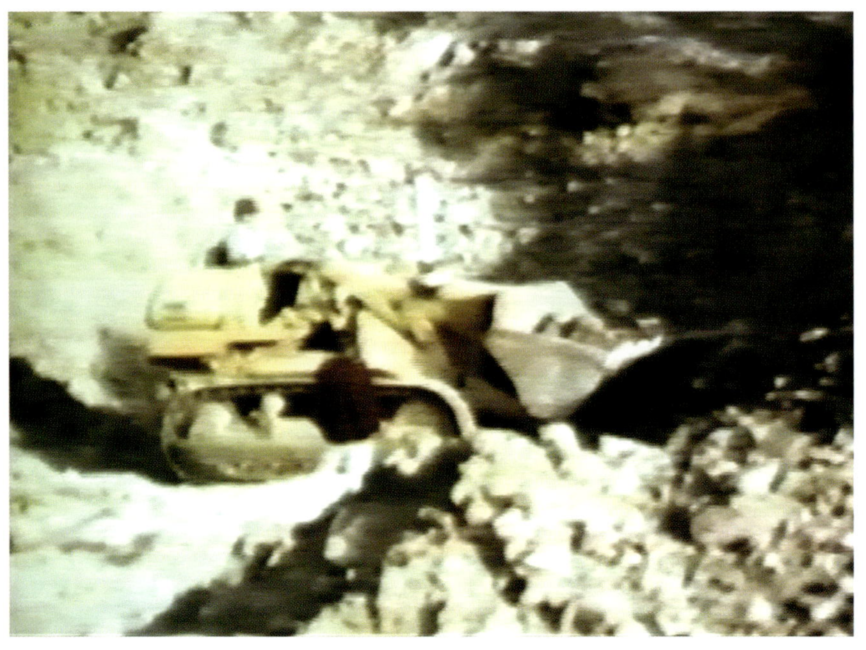

20.

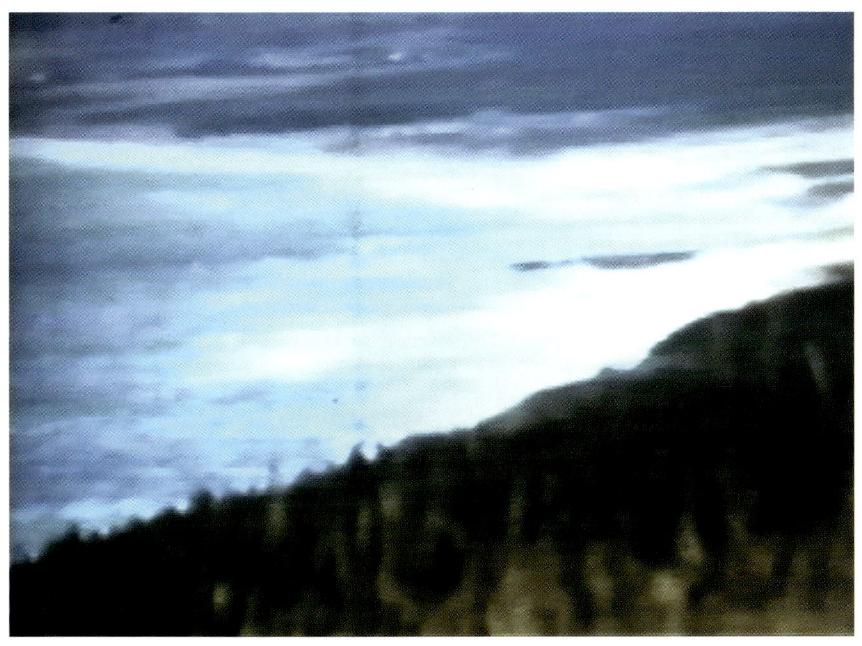

21.

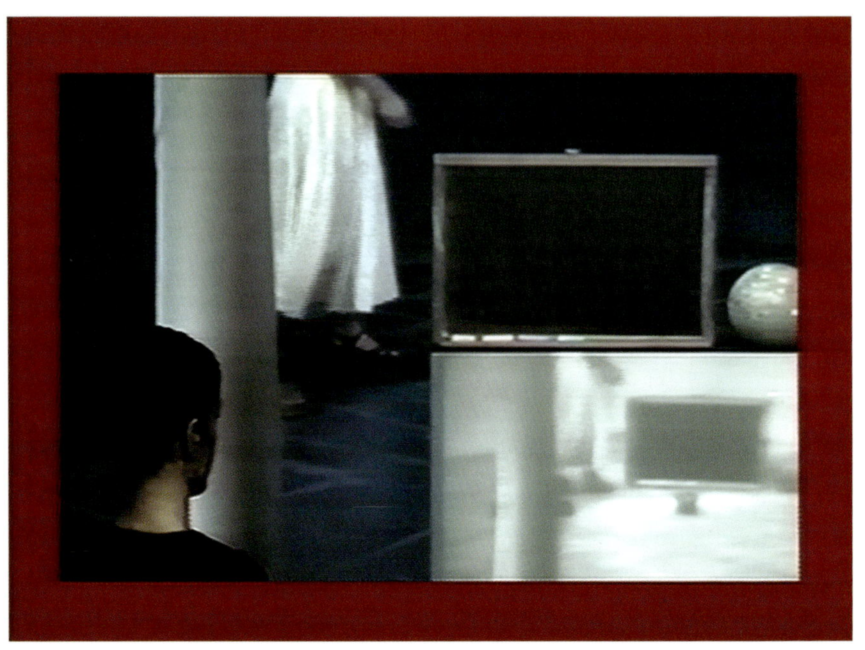

22.—24.

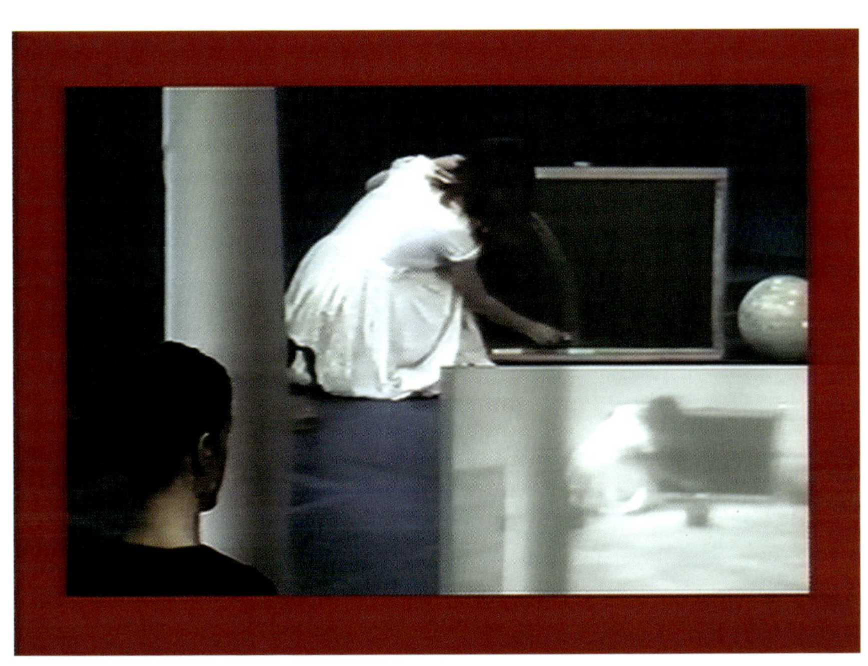

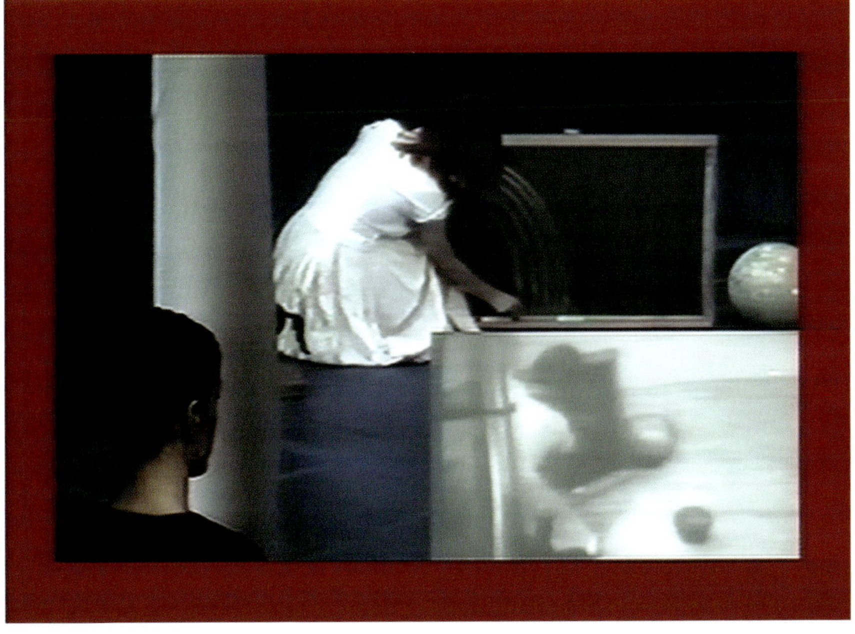

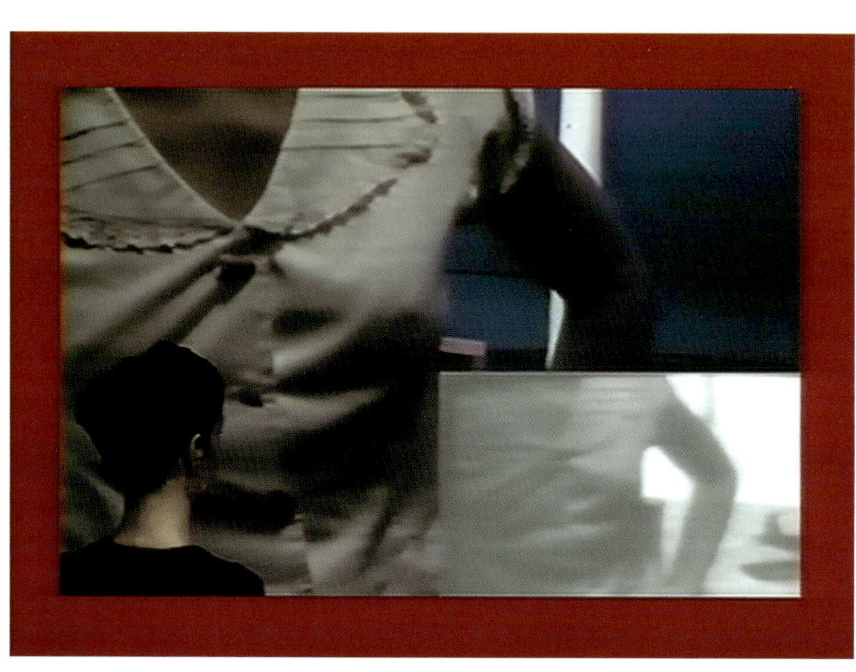

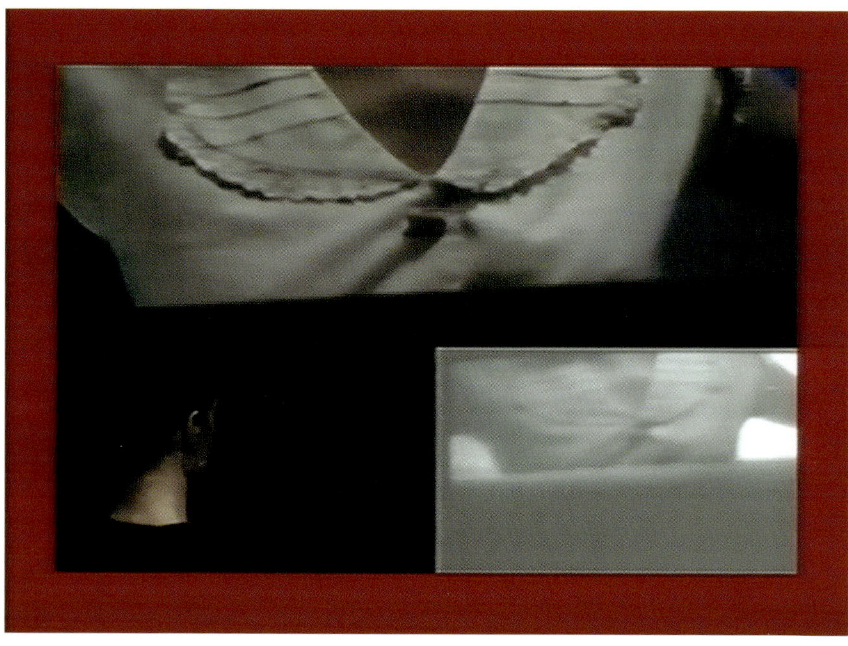

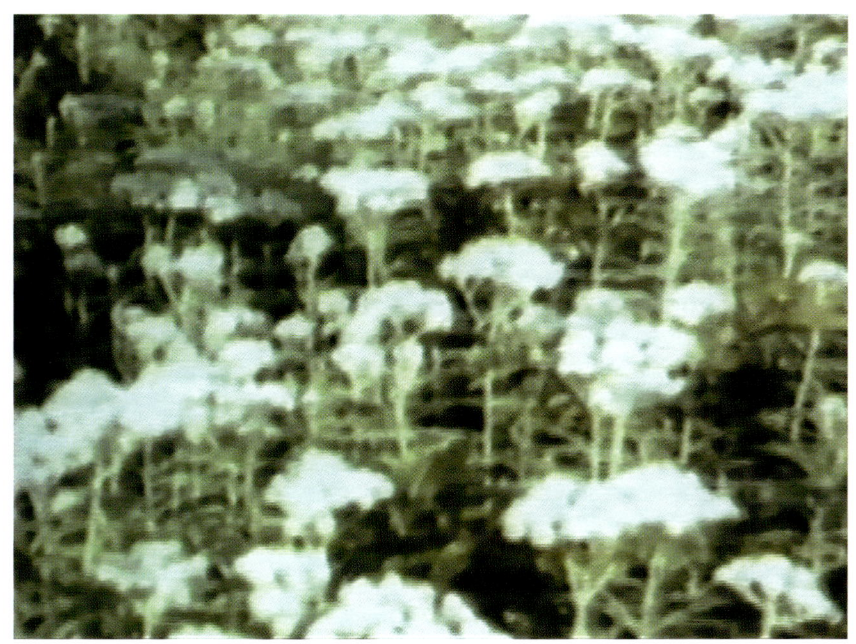

25.—27.

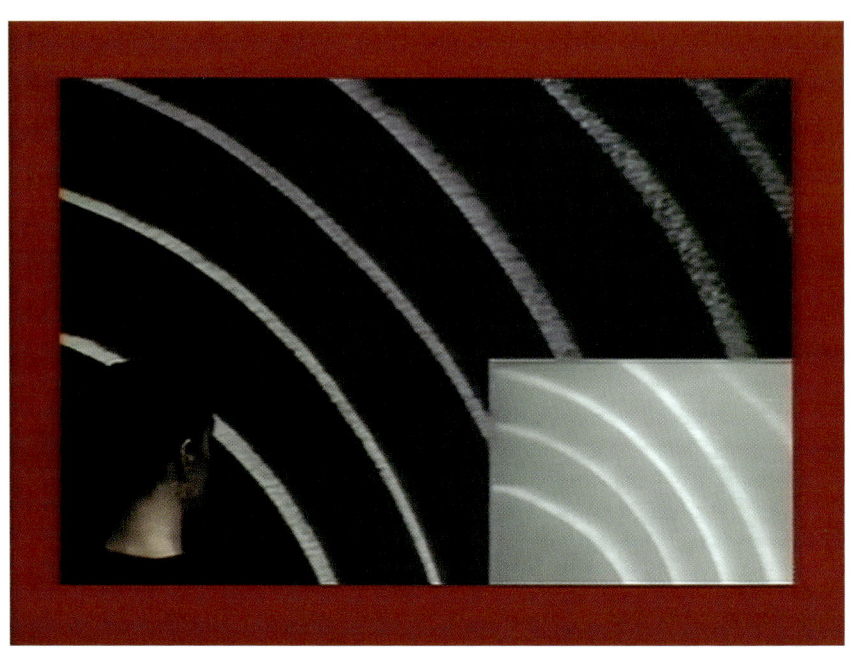

28.

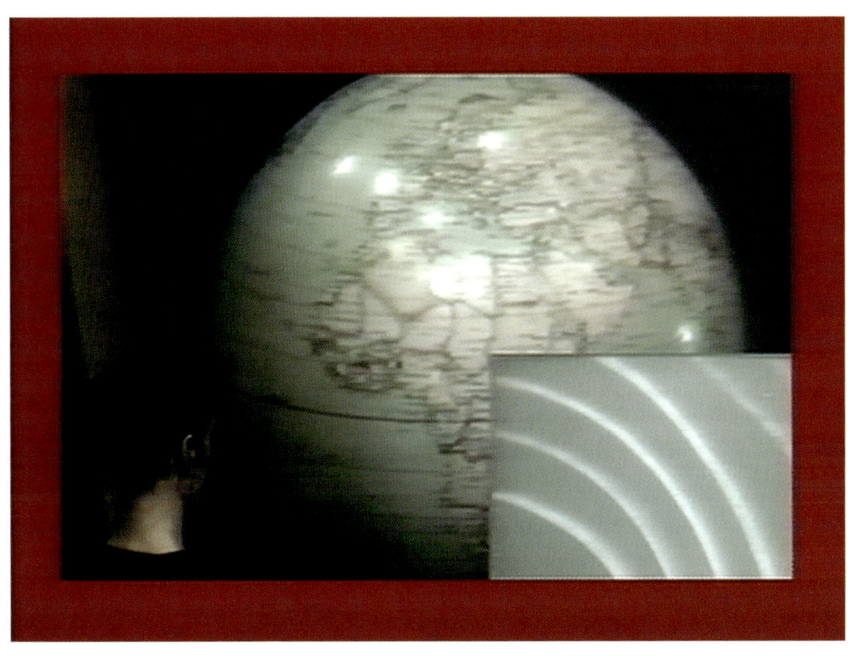

29.

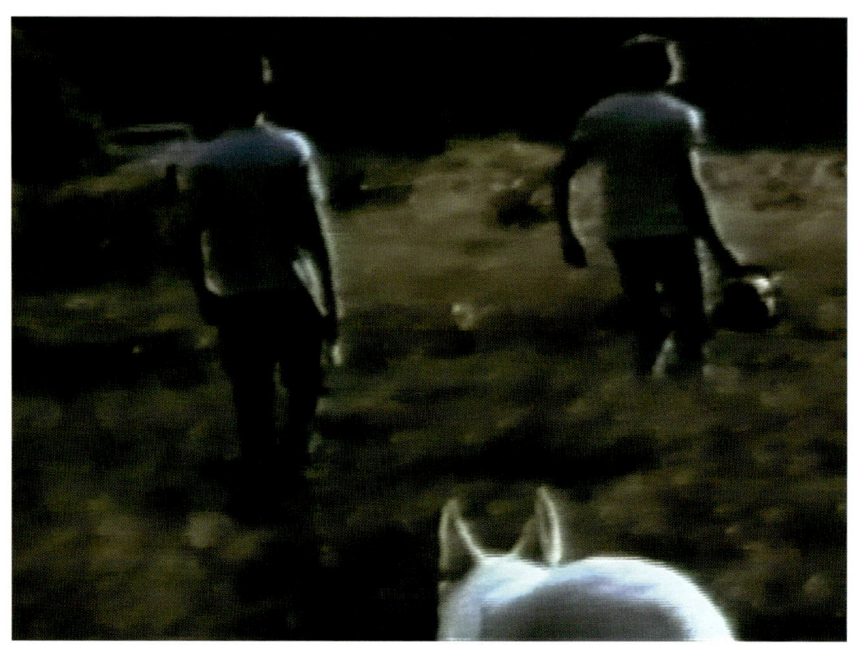

30.

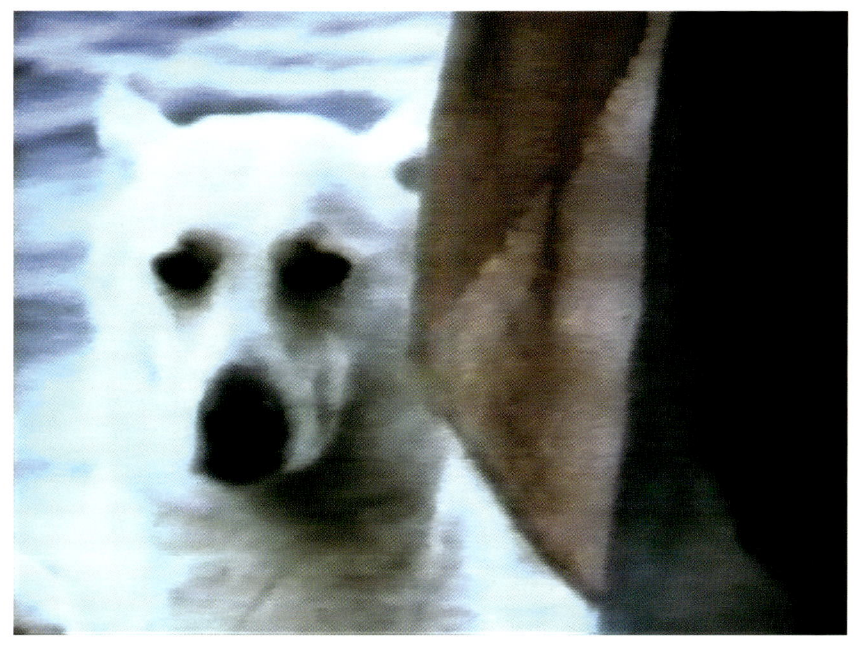

31.

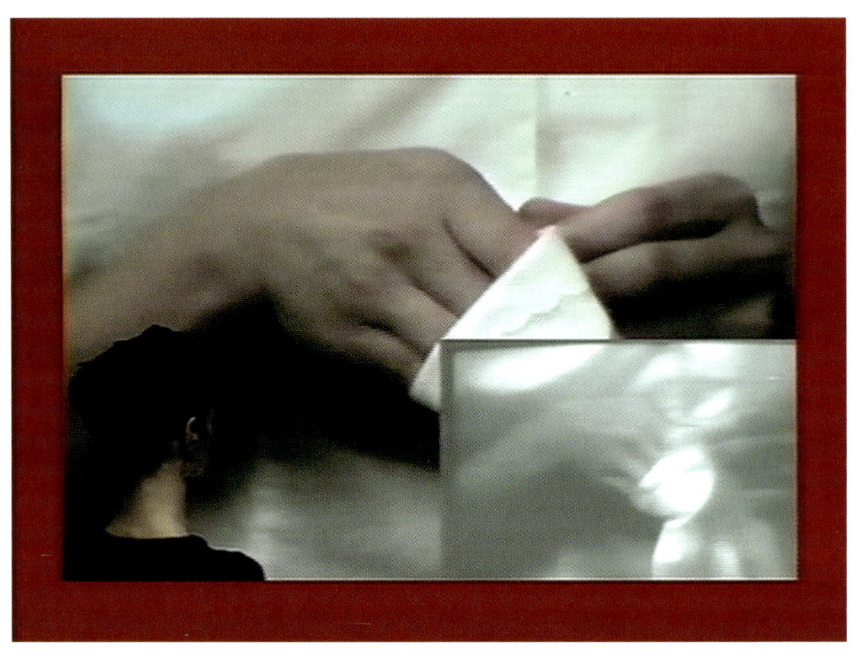

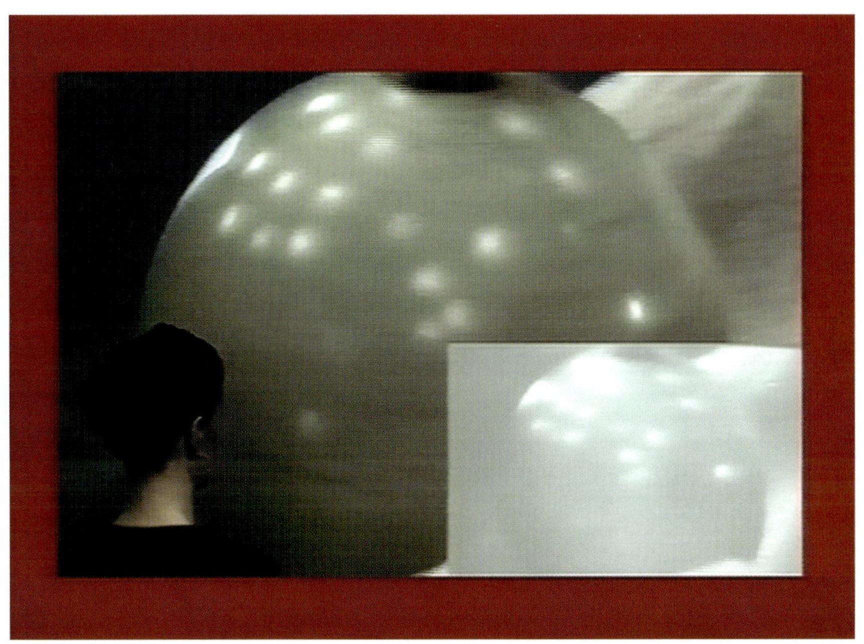

33.

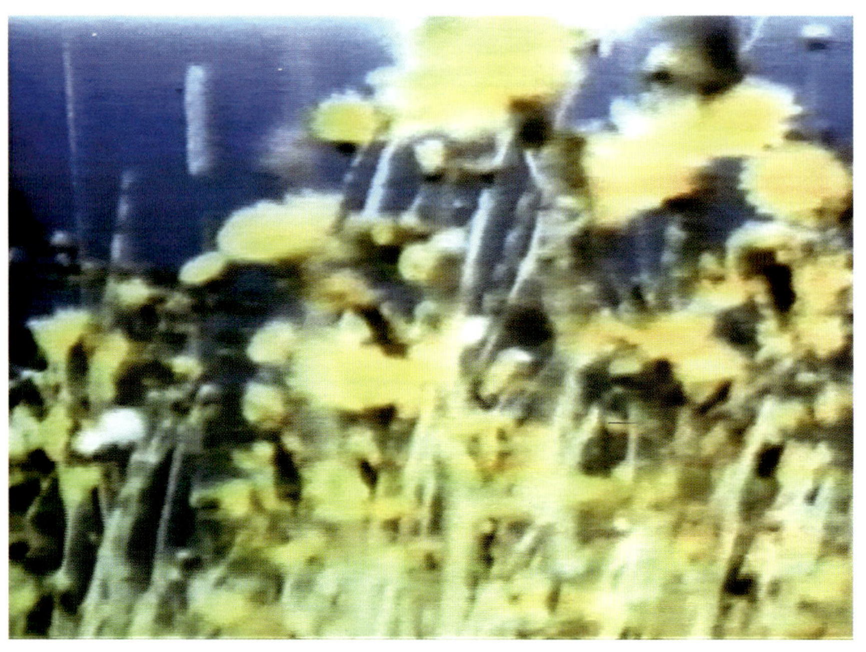

6min), a fragment of a film originally planned as part of a larger project. In Anger's film, the movie star (Yvonne Marquis, a name aglitter for the silver screen) is in full maquillage — spidery black false eyelashes and glistening scarlet lipstick — as she anoints herself before a cluttered dressing table. She shimmies into one transparent silk chiffon frock after another; sequins and beads shine and dance ecstatically in the light, like the dance of the seven veils filtered through vintage Hollywood glamour. Anger has referred to certain of his works as 'oneiric cinema': like a sorcerer's invocation of a dreamscape, he delivers a voluptuous fantasy realised in celluloid.[26]

For *Veil*, Jonas and Serra produced a series of 'wipes' — the filmic effect where a line moves across the screen, erasing the previous image and exposing a new one. Their 'wipes', however, are not produced using video technology. Rather, the effect is dismantled, hand-made. The illusion is revealed and the camera barely moves: a bamboo shade is lifted to reveal a pile of printed silks, velvets and fur; each layer of fabric is then whisked away, one after another, removed by Jonas's hands, just visible at the sides of the frame. As the final veil, a layer of luxurious fur, is removed, Jonas's face — eyes closed, soundless in a dream — is exposed.

When Sergei Eisenstein wrote about the theatre director Vsevolod Meyerhold, his mentor, he described a masterful conjurer capable of producing unsettling effects and astonishing images:

*His lectures were mirages and dreams… But one cannot
remember what Meyerhold said. Aromas, colours, sounds.
A golden haze over everything. Elusiveness, intangibility,
secret upon secret, secret upon secret, veil behind veil —
not seven of them, but eight, twelve, thirty, fifty!*[27]

Eisentein constructed his own films rhythmically
with a controlled flood and clash of images. Film,
as Jonas discovered, was a pliable, mysterious and
versatile material, a medium for creating multiple
images and magical transformations; and video —
inexpensive and immediate — presented a way to
approximate that experience.

Jonas has described her graduate school education as
being made up of university classes by day combined
with movie-going every other night.[28] In 1962, film-
maker/critic and peripatetic programmer Jonas Mekas,
who had been organising film screenings in New York
since 1952, helped found the Film-maker's Cooperative,
which begat the Film-maker's Cinematheque, and, in
1970, was established as the Anthology Film Archives.
Mekas's programmes — always dedicated to avant-garde,
independent, previously undistributed or under-shown
foreign films and expanded cinema — included films
by Dziga Vertov, Jean Vigo, Sergei Eisenstein, Maya
Deren, Robert Frank, Kenneth Anger and Jack Smith.[29]

When Jonas saw Jack Smith's mythopoeic films and
performances at the Cinematheque and other downtown
venues, she recognised their importance: his intoxicat-
ingly slow performances were a perpetual interplay

of live action, projected slides and films, spun out
of squalid glamour, hesitant gestures and the flicker
of light and shadows. Smith's performances were
protracted hypnotic ceremonies, confounding and
riveting: films were spliced with masking tape, the
record player would break down and slide images —
projected onto a screen improvised from a rumpled
sheet — appeared as luminous puddles spilling into
three dimensions. Visionary and grindingly low-tech,
this was inspired multimedia: dedicated to illusion
and underwhelmed by gadgetry, it deliriously subverted
any conventional idea of theatre or film.

In the interior vignettes of *I Want to Live in the
Country (And Other Romances)*, the woman in white
performs a variety of ordinary actions — pulling on
a pair of dainty white gloves, waving a fan, drawing
on a blackboard, jumping up from a chair, spinning a
globe — yet everything splinters and turns unfamiliar.
In one scene, she swings her skirt and the fabric
billows, buoyant and cloud-like. The woman's headless
torso dips into a slow *plié* while a solid black rectangle
rises up from the bottom of the screen and everything
disappears.

I Want To Live In The Country
The title appears against a black screen, in bright
white letters — all capitals and in a plain sans-serif
typeface — blunt and stark as a warning sign. 'I always
make my own titles, but this one — *I Want to Live in
the Country (And Other Romances)*,' Jonas wrote in a 2006
letter, 'is really the one exception. The title came from

a conversation with my old friend Charles Ruas.'[30]
A writer and editor as well as a noted translator, Ruas
was then director of arts programming at New York's
WBAI, a non-commercial, progressive radio station
regarded as the channel of information during the
protest era. Jonas and Ruas met in the mid—1960s,
through mutual friends Fanny and Susan Howe, two
sisters: Fanny is a poet and novelist and Susan a painter
turned poet who had been Jonas's fellow student at
The School of the Museum of Fine Arts in Boston.
'There was the most extraordinary energy and willing-
ness to experiment,' Susan Howe has recalled. 'Painters,
sculptors, dancers, filmmakers, musicians, conceptual
artists were all working together and crossing genre
boundaries...'[31]

There is a rich vein of abiding friendship that occurs
within Jonas's work; although distinctly individual,
her work is also amiably informed by an extended
community, a quiet reminder of how the exchange
of ideas — the offer of an unknown quote or reference
source, a technique, a familiar but critical eye, even
the lauded second opinion — informs and clarifies
what eventually becomes an artist's lone decision-
making process. Examples are not difficult to find:
the artist Rob Wynne (Ruas's partner, he was also the
musical director at WBAI) had advised Jonas on how
to establish tension between image and music, creating
an opposition of sound and visuals, a fugue for video;
in 2001, when Jonas was invited to make a new work
for Documenta 11 based on an epic poem, it was Susan
Howe who suggested *Helen in Egypt*, a 1961 book-length

epic written by H.D. (Hilda Doolittle) that provided
one of the central sources for Jonas's multimedia
performance *Lines in the Sand* (Kassel, 2002).[32]

Jonas has remarked:

The people I performed for in the 70s were all friends.
My performance would change from night to night or
from one month to the next as a result of making it for
the audience. The art world then was almost like a workshop.
We worked for each other and we appreciated each other's
work. We talked to each other about our work.[33]

Jonas's outdoor performance works, made between
1970 and 1972, were, in fact, enacted by groups of people,
art-world non-performers and a sprinkling of dancers.
According to Jonas, it was:

Always people I knew. Among them were Frances Barth,
Simone Forti, Jene Highstein, Gordon Matta-Clark,
Judy Padow, Janelle Reiring, Susan Rothenberg,
George Trakas, Jackie Winsor. At the same time, I liked
to give performances for my closest friends.

Since 1970, Jonas — who lives in New York and works
throughout the world — has spent summers in Canada's
Atlantic maritime provinces: on the western coast
of Cape Breton Island and the northern highlands
of Nova Scotia. Phillip Glass, writing in his career
memoir, tells the story of how he and theatre director/
writer JoAnne Akalaitis left New York with their first
child in 1969 and looked for a place to work during the

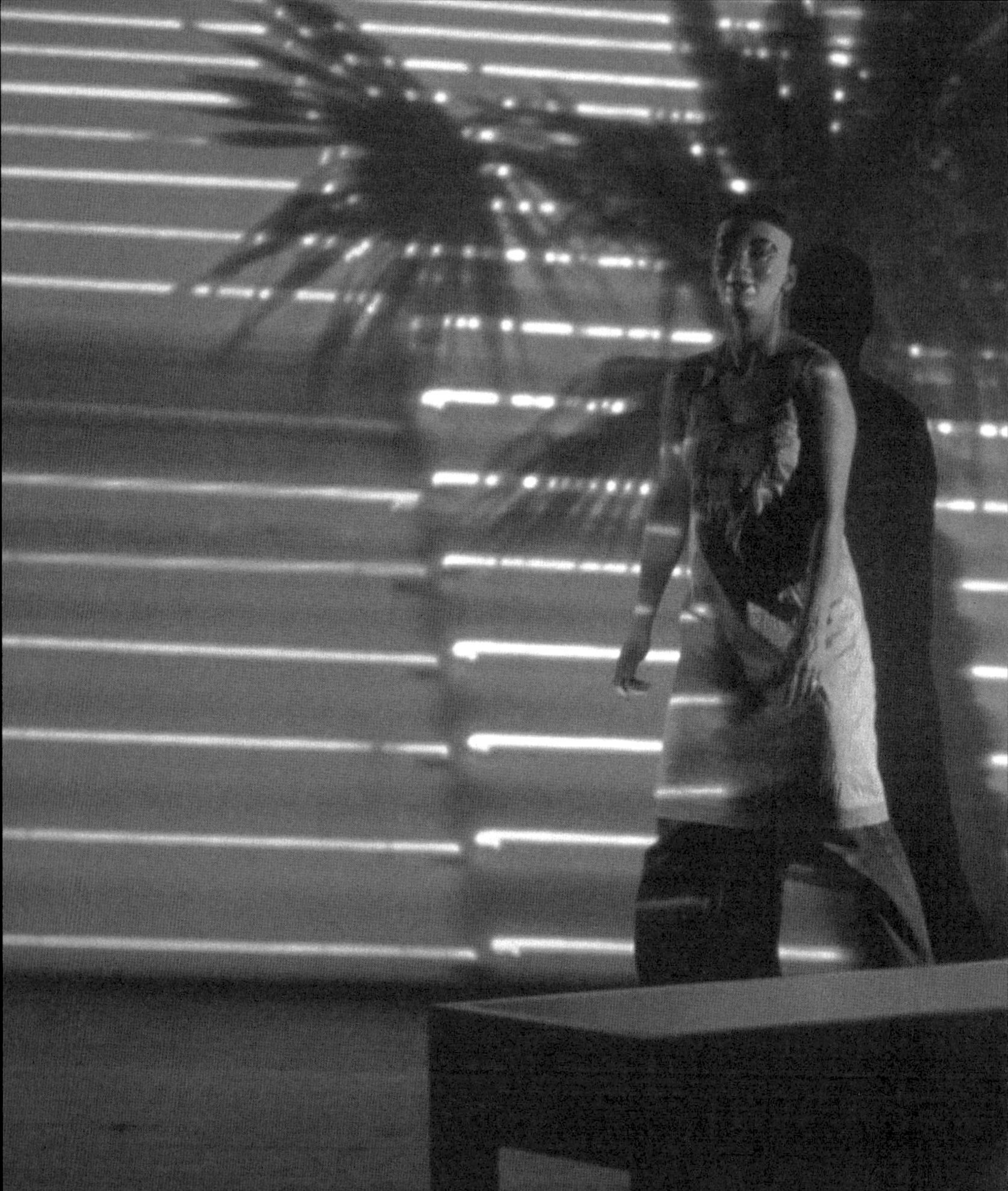

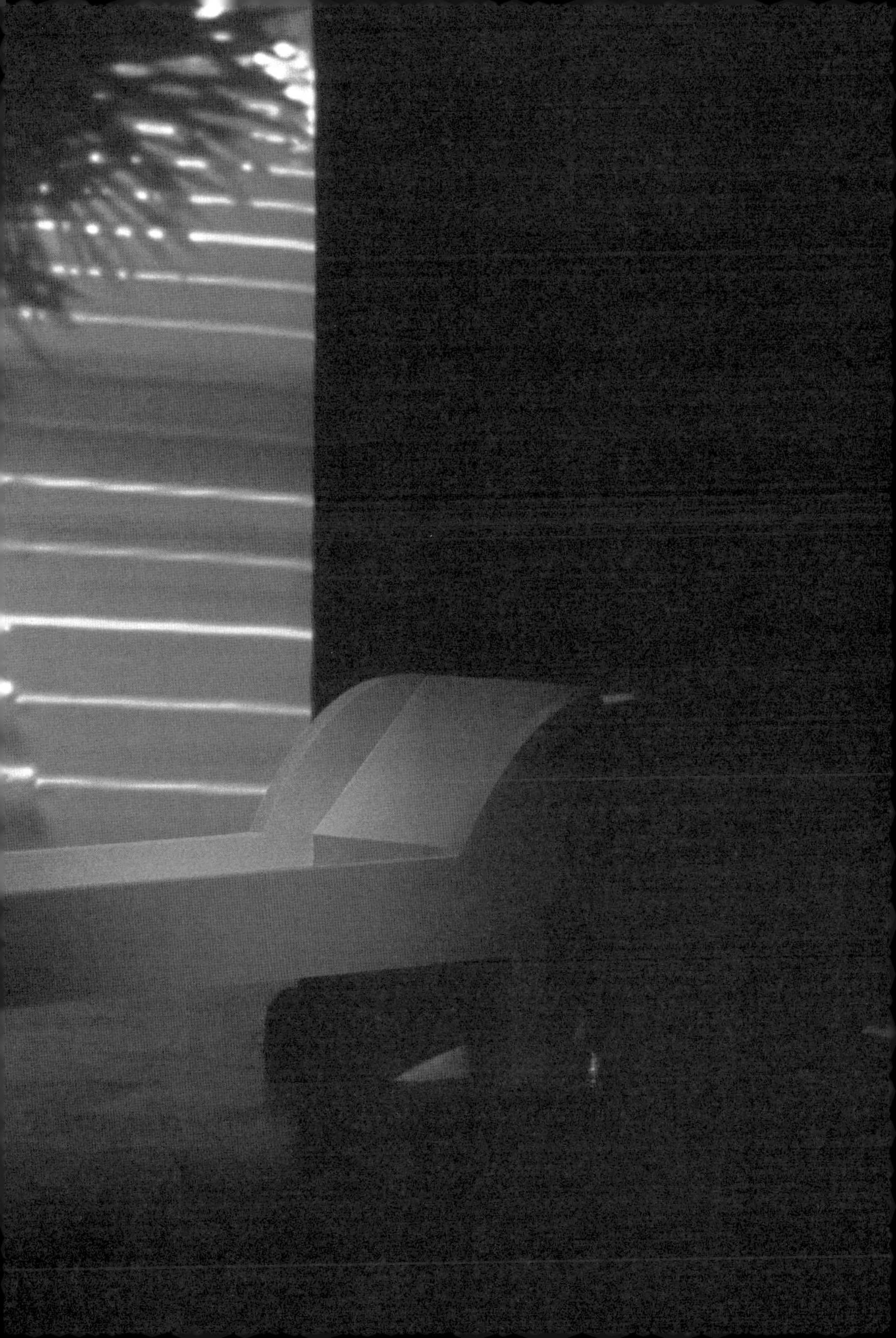

summers. They started their search along the Atlantic
coast of Maine and ended up in Cape Breton. With a
friend, writer Rudy Wurlitzer, they bought a property
that Glass says is best described in travel-agent prose:
'an abandoned summer camp on a cliff overlooking
the sea, containing a sprawling main lodge, a handful
of log shacks buried in an expanse of pine forest, a
vast and bleakly beautiful stretch of beach. Satisfyingly
remote.'[34] This is the very landscape — the seaside
cliffs, the piney woods — that appears in *I Want to
Live in the Country (And Other Romances)*.

Cape Breton, with its rugged shoreline, barren headlands
and broad valleys, is reminiscent, in many ways, of
Scotland. There is also a historical Scottish influence
to this region: during the Highland Clearances that
persisted from 1745 until the middle of the nineteenth
century, thousands of Scottish tenant farm families
— who had been violently removed from their land and
sent into forced migration — resettled in Cape Breton.
That past can be heard in the present: in the music
played at local ceilidhs and more occasionally in
the spoken Gaelic language. It's a curious phenomenon
— the way that cultural information is preserved
in immigrant communities and isolated places, like a
vestige of history in amber. Cape Breton is a place where
the old world and new are finely layered together and
folk culture flourishes in the gap between art and life.
It is a place after Jonas's heart.

'Most of the young, I am sure, imagine that they
thought it up [abandoning the city for country living]

out of their own heads, just as they imagine they
invented pacifism, sit-ins, self-reliance, participatory
democracy, progressive education and sexual freedom,'
wrote social critic Paul Goodman in his introduction
to the 1970 popular reissue of Helen and Scott Nearing's
*Living the Good Life: How to Live Safely and Sanely
in a Troubled World.*[35] The Nearings, peace activists,
conservationists and counter-culture role models,
left New York City in 1932 to homestead a Vermont
farm. Scott Nearing had been an economics professor
and Helen a violinist and theosophist, an intimate
of Krishnamurti; their account of country living
examines economic possibilities, philosophical
and societal questions and historical antecedents.
Although their book was not unrealistically romantic
or theoretically abstract, it was able to speak
(as Goodman begrudgingly admits) to an idealistic
generation, in the heyday of *The Whole Earth Catalog*,
who dreamed of practical utopias and going back
to the land.

Interior: the cropped image of the woman in white is
cropped even further, made smaller, distilled to gestures.
Her elbows are held in close to her waist, and only her
forearms and hands are visible. Most often we see only
her hands set against the bright, blue background and
the uninterrupted whiteness of her dress. The hands
perform a little dance, pulling on a pair of white gloves.
The fingers interlace, splay and tug at the fabric. The
woman in white delicately twiddles her gloved hands.
On the soundtrack, dogs are barking. The voiceover remains
uninflected, but the language reveals a wariness: 'When

I saw the man with the red car at the fire, the mystery escaped. But my obsession continues. It's the distant figure on the hill. The house in the future. And the man in the distance.' On the screen, the left hand wriggles into an immaculate white glove with a very tiny bow, barely visible, adorning the wrist. 'But he thinks I should have a trailer and a gun,' continues the voiceover.

Robert Frank with June Leaf also bought land on this edge of Cape Breton in the summer of 1969. As Frank then wrote: 'We build a building, overlooking the sea. I spend a lot of time looking out the window. Camera still in the closet. I wait.'[36] Living with the land is a prospect that is equally alluring and overwhelming. In 1975, Frank made a film called *Keep Busy* (16mm, black-and-white, 38min). Shot on Sea Wolf Island from a bare-bones script; written by novelist Rudy Wurlitzer (screenwriter for *Two Lane Black Top*, Monte Hellman's existential American road movie that featured a souped-up '55 Chevy and unaffected, quietly charismatic performances), *Keep Busy* is an ambiguous, partly improvised story obviously inspired by Samuel Beckett. The film's performers, actors and non-actors, include Joan Jonas, Richard Serra, JoAnne Akalaitis, June Leaf, David Warrilow, Bill Raymond and Roberta Neiman as islanders living on the brink of the world.

Keep Busy is set on an isolated island dotted forlornly with a few tumbledown shacks and a white-washed lighthouse. 'Nobody except us,' remarked Frank during the filming. 'Very poetic calm — in the middle of the

water and hundreds of seagulls — and for a few days
we could see a great number of whales pass very close
to the island.'[37] Jonas remembers being stranded on
the island for three days. 'It was fun,' she says with
wry amusement.[38] In *Keep Busy* a ragged assortment
of people struggle in the harsh landscape. A lighthouse
keeper talks obliquely about time, the past and the
approaching winter. The cast of islanders shuffle
about in big rubber boots, obsessed with the dailiness of
their lives, battling inclement weather and undertaking
futile tasks. Wurlizter has described the film's
interplay of fiction and non-fiction:

*What interested me was questioning where the boundaries
of fiction lie and where the margins are, how to use reality
on one level and fictional approach on the other. They
mutated where you use them together.*[39]

One of the exterior scenes of *I Want to Live in the Country
(And Other Romances)* opens with a shot of a window,
hung with a sheer white curtain, upstairs in a grey
shingled house. The camera lingers for a few seconds
there, then drops down and away, brushing quickly
over treetops, down into a field and across toward the
sea. Cows are lowing. We catch sight of another house,
a barn. 'Time is more precious year by year,' reads the
voiceover. 'The air sharper. The sun warmer. And the
trees more like friends. And my friends more precious,
like trees.'

The voiceover text that accompanies *I Want to Live in the
Country (And Other Romances)* was culled from journal

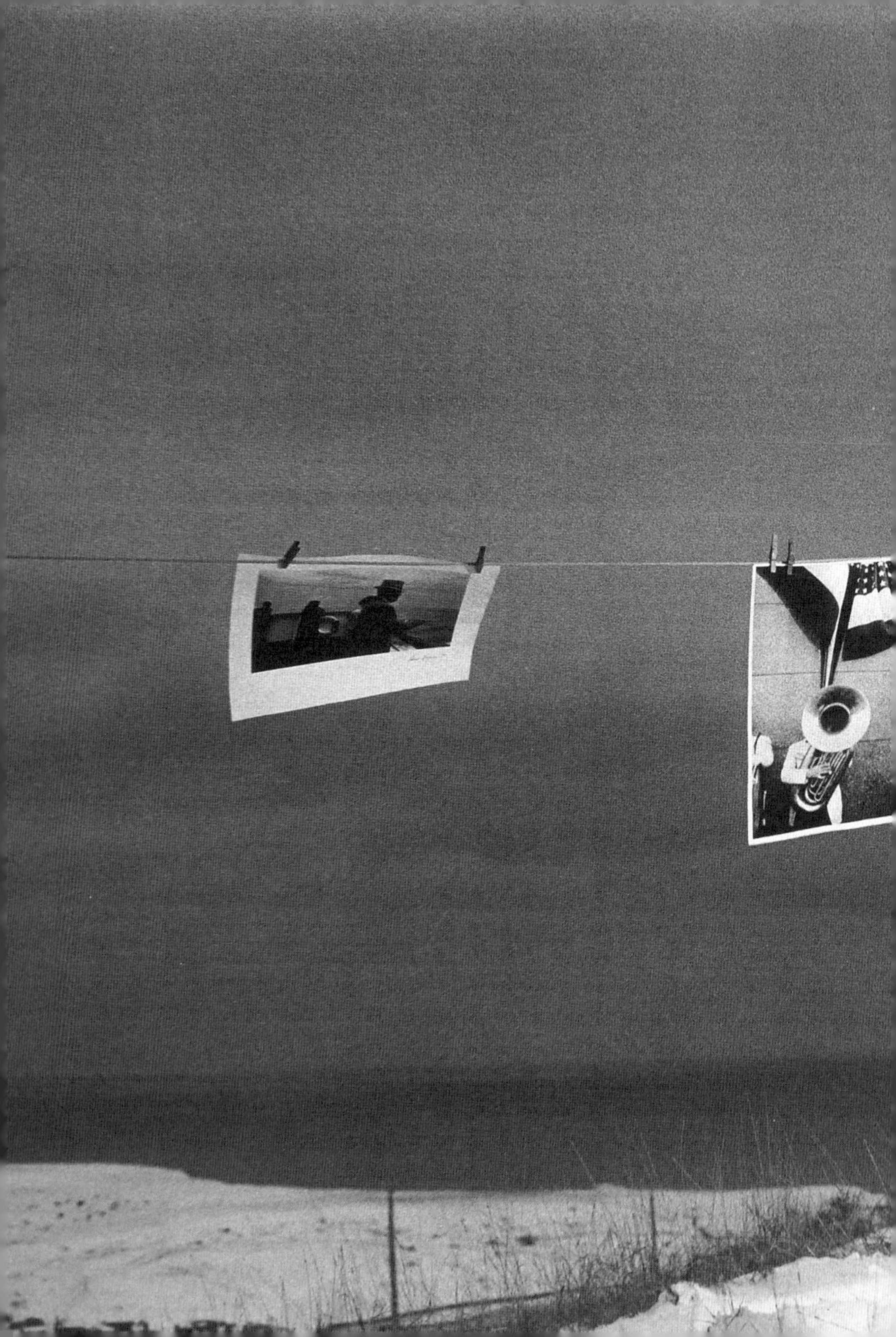

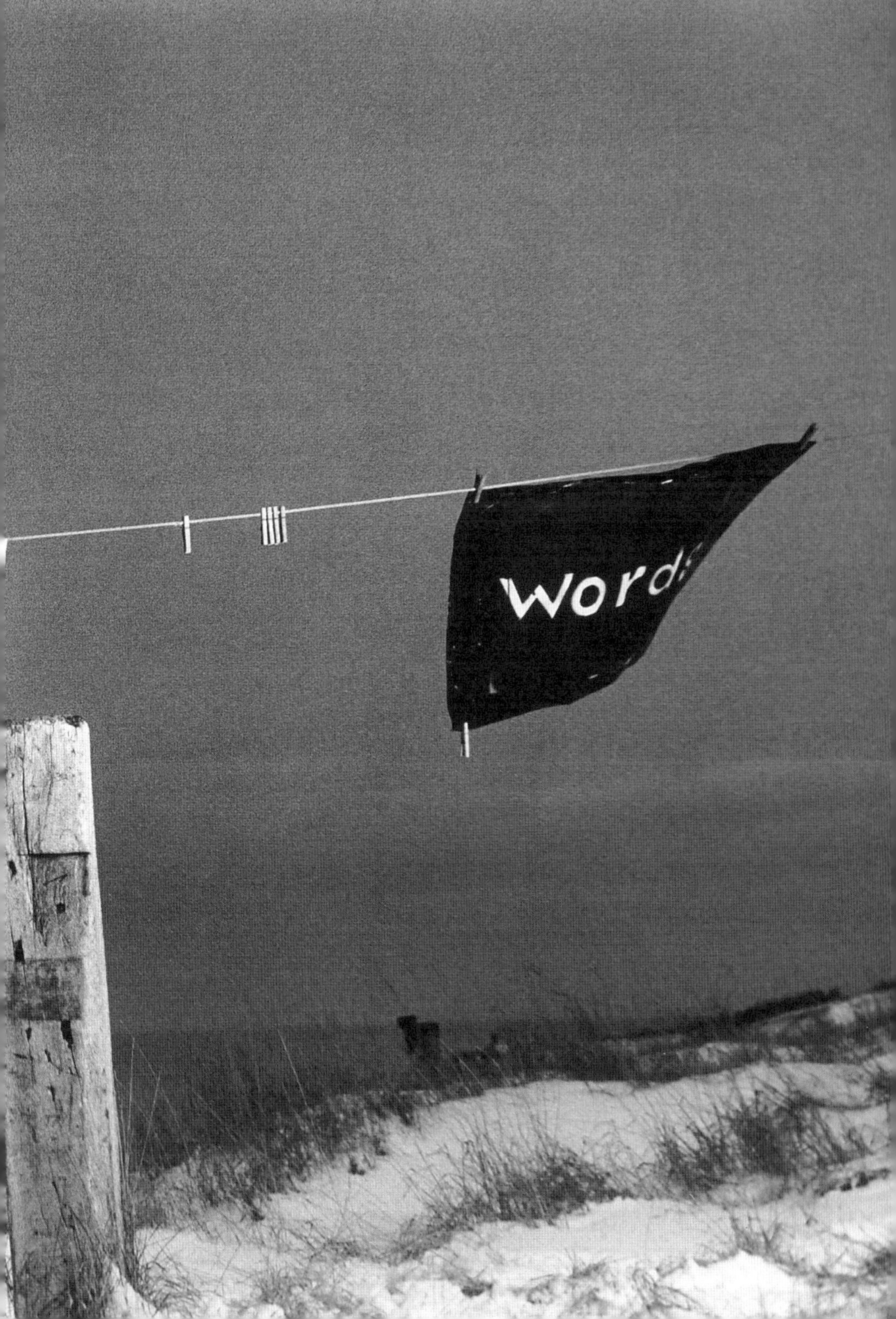
word

entries that Jonas made during one Cape Breton
summer. For this, her first video to feature a text,
Jonas did all the writing. 'I knew I was going to use
the journal,' Jonas has explained. 'So I was writing
about the events of the day in a self-conscious way.
But there is still a simplicity about it.'[40] The text,
like the images, is evocative and thoughtfully
considered, but also consciously fragmented. Even
though Jonas once demurred that 'she never learned
to write', she has always been a keen observer and
an ardent reader, receptive and discerning about both
the rhythms and allusive power of language. 'My work
is really something made for the public,' Jonas has
stated. 'I never want it to be described as autobiographical.'[41] It's a vernacular text considering ideas and an
actual place, but never confessing details of the artist's
life. Informed by references (visible and invisible)
to literature and mythology, Jonas's texts and images
are composed to stand alone, 'I was finding a language
of forms, a way of telling my friends a story in
pictures.'[42] Fiction and non-fiction.

Jonas told me that *I Want to Live in the Country
(And Other Romances)* was always the title of the
work. 'It was not an addition,' she wrote me recently
when I asked when '(And Other Romances)' had been
added to the title. I like the way the parenthetical
afterthought seems to topple the bold declaration,
pushing 'I Want to Live in the Country' into a widening
pool of possibilities. 'It was from the start just what
it is,' Jonas wrote in her response.[43] The tape I own
is labelled *I Want to Live in the Country (And Other*

Romances), but when the tape is viewed, the title
comes up only as *I Want To Live in the Country*.
For me, it works either way.

The white-on-black title card presents the sentence
parsed in two, neat as a minimalist stack: 11 letters
— **I WANT TO LIVE** — placed solidly on top of 12
— **IN THE COUNTRY**. It's a title that delivers a
concise kick, brusque as a marquee for a 1950s Susan
Hayward melodrama ('I Want to Live!' or 'I'll Cry
Tomorrow'), desirous but not clamouring. On the second
title card, there is one credit, divided into two lines:
BY / JOAN JONAS.

Exterior: the camera crawls along close to the ground,
a sun-dappled haze of green and yellow. The two white
dogs sit up, alert, posed in silhouette. Their heads pivot.
'It is very quiet,' says the voiceover. 'The sun is setting
and there is something quietly crashing in the woods.'
A dog is barking offscreen and the pair onscreen swing
their heads around silently, looking. 'Maybe it is an
animal or the boy who is making a path to the flat rock.
She calls his name and the noise stops immediately.
And does not resume.' The camera pulls back along the
verdant ground; a pale, quivering green floods the screen.

Although Jonas's work is entranced by film, literature
— along with ritual, transformation and the love of
magic — is also at the heart of her practice. Among her
earliest performances, *Mirror Piece I* (first performed
at the Loeb Student Centre, New York University in 1969)
and *Mirror Piece II, Mirror Check* (Emanu-El, YMHA,

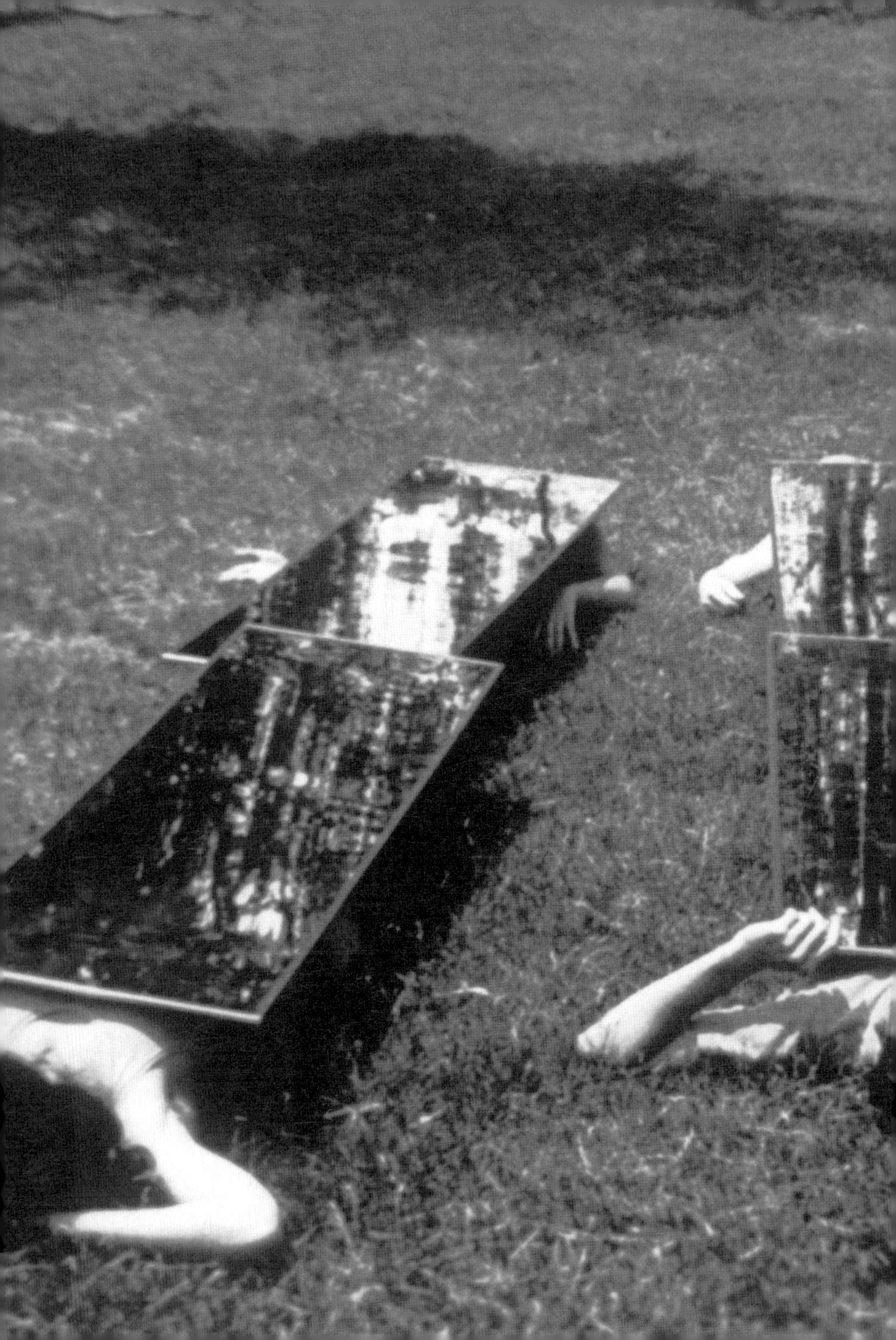

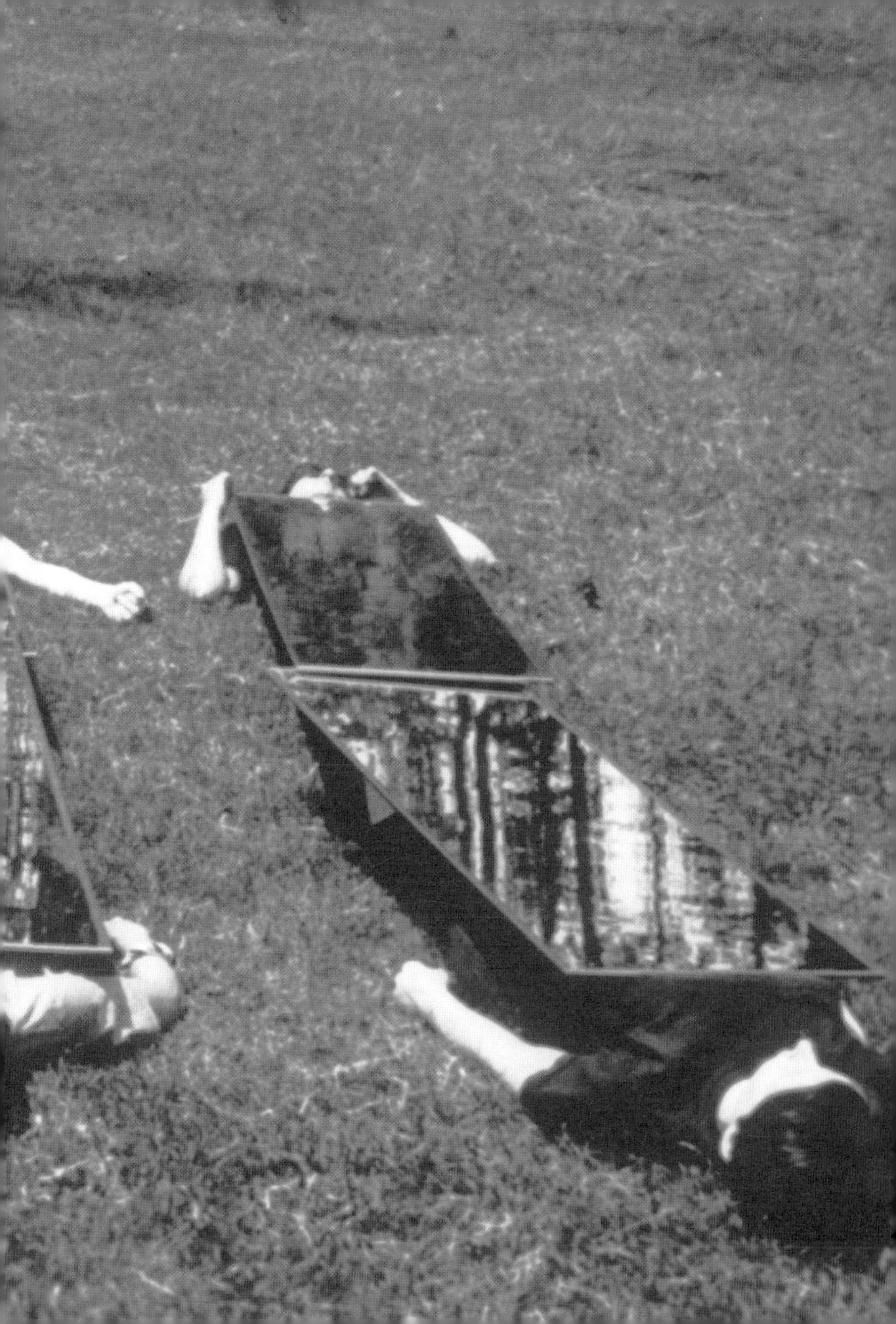

New York, 1970) was directly inspired by Jorge
Luis Borges's story collection *Labyrinths* (1964).
As a group of performers, carrying full-length mirrors,
moved trepidatiously across the floor, Jonas read
all the references to mirrors that feature in
Borges's book.

In *I Want to Live in the Country (And Other Romances)*
the video monitor that appears in the lower right-hand
corner acts as a mirror; the videotapes that play there
reflect and reverse, in distorted time and incomplete
images, the scenes that occur in the studio. Sometimes
a mirror is placed in the background of the set and
the image of the entire room is duplicated again.
'We found another white dog like the first. She had
chased a sheep over a cliff,' says the voiceover while
the image of a woman's hand slowly waving a folded
fan nearly fills the screen. 'I became uneasy when
he told me how much it would cost. Where should
it go? I drew the hills again and again.' There is only
the hint of a story followed unpredictably by a concern,
a question, a remark.

The woman's hand continues to languidly wave the fan,
suggesting a slight breeze in the airless room. In Noh
theatre a folding fan is an essential and versatile prop
that can stand in for a cup, paper, pen, sword — or a
dozen other roles. Jonas gave an antique European fan,
gold-tipped and decorated with images of eighteenth-
century ladies, to Organic Honey as part of her trove
of feminine wiles. In *I Want to Live in the Country
(And Other Romances)*, when a painted folding fan

appears, it bows toward the camera and reveals its blank, unpainted backside. Disembodied and centre stage, the fluttering hand-held fan is reflected in the mirror; like a dancer in a rehearsal hall, each one of its performed gestures is doubled, intensified and narcissistically demanding attention.

Borges claimed a life-long fear of mirrors. 'The earliest fears and wonders of my childhood,' he said. 'Being afraid of mirrors, being afraid of mahogany, being afraid of being repeated.'[44] As an adult he expressed his fear, or at least a dislike and distrust, for cameras — a variation on his fear of mirrors, he believed. In *Labyrinths*, the spiraling labyrinth endlessly redoubling is the ultimate mirror.

In his 1939 essay, 'When Fiction Lives in Fiction', Borges recalled a childhood fascination: gazing at the picture on top of a biscuit tin that showed a picture of the biscuit tin, in an infinite regress of biscuit tins. He compares the experience to the destabilising *en abyme* of looking at Diego Velázquez's painting *Las Meninas*, or reading the dimension-defying fiction of Flann O'Brien. 'The pictorial technique of inserting a painting within a painting,' writes Borges, 'corresponds, in the world of letters, to the interpolation of a fiction within another fiction.'[45] In *I Want to Live in the Country (And Other Romances)*, Jonas creates an unreal space, an imagined room, and then documents it: an ephemeral scene is preserved — false, but as stubbornly ongoing as history.

At MIT, where Jonas has taught since 2000, she once
asked her students to bring in their favorite scene
from a film. Jonas chose Fellini's *Nights of Cabiria*
(1957) and a scene titled 'The Mesmerist'.[46] Cabiria
(Giulietta Masina) walks into the Lux music hall and
brusquely demands to know if the show is any good.
'You want me to say it stinks?', the ticket seller spits
back. Cabiria buys her ticket and joins a miserable
audience of boisterous single men and one amorous
couple. Before them, a top-hatted magician performs
with two lovely assistants dressed for the *seraglio*.
The magician invites the sceptical Cabiria to join
him onstage. She bristles, he cajoles, she joins him.
He takes off his top hat and devil's horns spring from
his head. He removes the horns and is transformed
again, into a maestro in white tie and tails. Just as
Cabiria, embarrassed and still belligerent, is about
to flee the stage, the magician waves his hand over
her head. A gong strikes. The air trembles. She is
mesmerised. Her face, tense as a hard little fist,
suddenly softens. She is radiant, lovely. In a trance,
she begins to pick imaginary flowers. A spotlight
follows her, a funnel of brightness illuminating her
head. The magician gingerly crowns her with a halo
of flowers. She waltzes blissfully on tip-toe, lost
in a dream. 'Is it really true?', she asks, full of hope,
enchanted. 'Do you really love me?' A tinny cymbal
is struck and she collapses. In the imaginary world
of a film, a woman goes to a magic show and slips
into her own dream: a fiction occurs within a fiction,
in an infinite regress.

While a graduate student at Columbia University
Jonas studied American poetry with F.W. Dupee,
a jaunty, rueful critic and one-time literary editor
at the Marxist publication *New Masses* (1926 — 1948),
who was significant to an earlier generation of
New York intellectuals.[47] Jonas's reading there
focused on twentieth-century American writers
— H.D. (Hilda Doolittle), the early poems and essays
of Ezra Pound and William Carlos Williams —
and the imagist tradition of poetry that was
exacting and vivid. In *Sea Garden*, a 1916 volume
of H.D.'s poetry, her poem titled 'The Wind Sleepers'
opens:

WHITER
than the crust
left by the tide,
we are stung by the hurled sand
and the broken shells.

We no longer sleep
in the wind —
we awoke and fled
through the city gate.[48]

H.D.'s unadorned language still feels entirely modern.
Each line is so spare, focused and evocative that it
becomes clear that a poem (even the quoted fragment
here) can have an undeniable physical presence and
prompt a picture in the mind's eye. In H.D.'s finely
constructed work, the words and lines are minimal
and dynamic. As Jonas wrote in a 1983 statement about

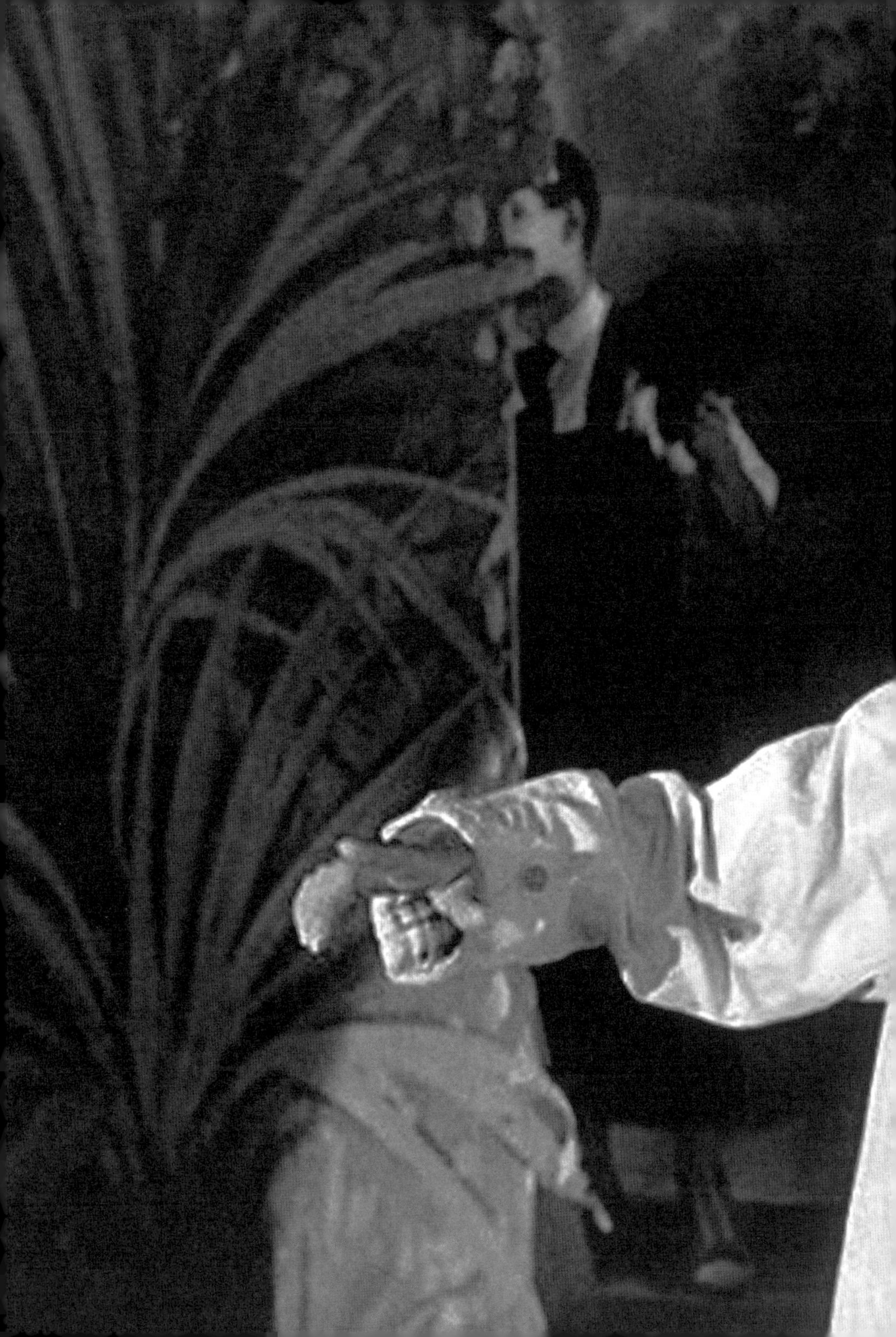

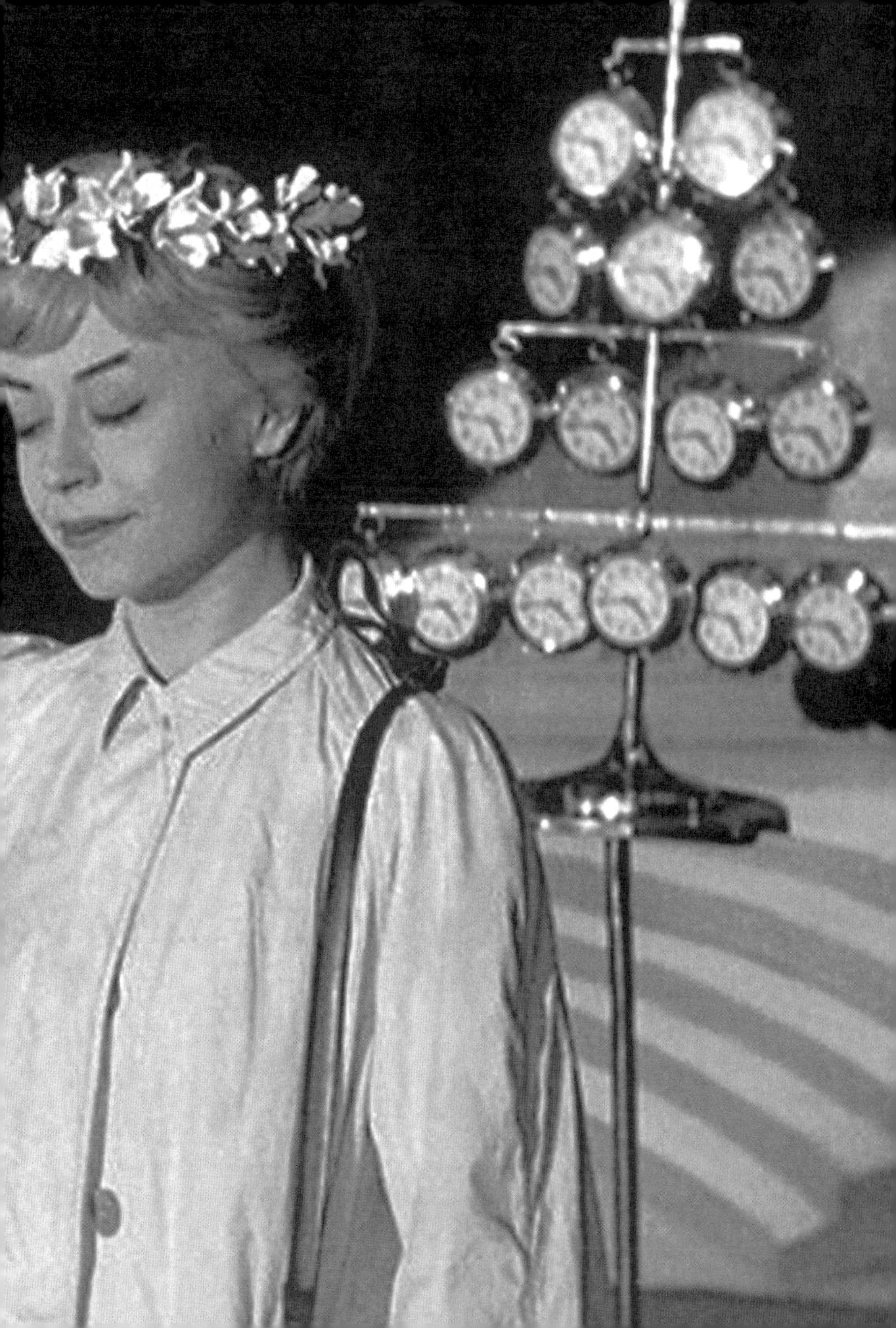

her own work: 'I didn't see a major difference between
a poem, a sculpture, a film or a dance.'[49]

The voiceover narration of *I Want to Live in the Country
(And Other Romances)* is as straightforward and potent
as one of H.D.'s imagist poems. Jonas's words are
attentive and carefully chosen. In one filmed sequence,
the screen is filled with scraggly stalks of yellow
wildflowers photographed against a bright sky.
The camera is low and still, a dog's eye-view looking
through the field. The image is a vibrating pattern
of nothing but flowers and sky; the colours are highly
contrasted and intense, but natural, unlike the blue
screen studio. The day is sunny and cloudless. The only
sound is the whistling of a high wind, a distant gale,
an approaching storm. We cannot see the ocean. 'The
water was slate grey and absolutely calm,' says the
voiceover. 'The sky was dark with patches of grey
light like sections of the sea. They came to visit and
I was relieved. They stayed until dark. It is silent and
ominous like something will happen.' Although the
text for *I Want to Live in the Country (And Other Romances)*
was written as a journal, the work is never memoir.
In the voiceover narration, the voice is always the same
one, while the pronouns shift: I, she, you, we. 'I woke
terrified,' says the unflappable voiceover. 'Later in the
dream,' the voiceover continues, 'she sat on the floor
of the ocean.'

At times, the images and the journal entries seem to
fall together harmoniously, and there is a lull that
is steady and straightforward as a bedtime story. More

often though, the promise of a story remains elusive, fractured. In a black-and-white filmed sequence, a pair of young white dogs (Sappho and Inook) frolic in the countryside. With their eyes and upturned lips outlined in inky black and their noses like lumps of coal, they have the look of exuberantly happy pups pictured in a children's book. Their ears perk up smartly as they nuzzle one another. The voiceover recounts:

Every day with the dogs, she walked into the woods with no path and charted another part in her memory with broken twigs, stalks and stems. She remembered summers long ago when she spent days alone in the trees.

For a very brief moment, a woman (painter Pat Steir) — dark-haired and wearing sunglasses — appears with the dogs. A white dog often be seen in Jonas's videotapes and drawings: the dog is her own dog merrily doubling as a mythic animal helper, an archetypal symbol of instinct. The dogs return in other vignettes. The dark-haired woman vanishes.

When Jonas first visited Japan in 1970, she was looking for an alternative language for art-making, 'one beyond Minimalism'. Encountering Noh theatre — with its slow tempo and use of rhythm, refined ritual and static gestures — she saw a complex and viable alternative. 'To try and watch the tempo grow,' observes Donald Richie, the great chronicler of Japanese culture, writing about Noh theatre. 'is like trying to watch the hour hand of the clock move, like trying to watch flowers open.'[50] Like the wedding ceremony performed in the mountains

of Crete, there are Noh performances — enacted for
marriages, memorial services for the dead and the
initiations of the shoguns — that go on for days. The
tradition of Noh theatre, dating back to the fourteenth
century and preserved through the revolution of 1868,
is a lyric drama of masks, the art of allusion and the
evocative power of associations. The Harvard-educated
Orientalist Ernest Fenollosa, whose translations and
notes on Noh plays were assembled posthumously by
Ezra Pound in 1913, has observed:

*The beauty and power of Noh lie in the concentration. All
elements — costume, motion, verse and music — unite to
produce a single clarified impression. Each drama embodies
some primary human relation or emotion; and the poetic
sweetness or poignancy of this is carried to its highest degree
by carefully excluding all such obtrusive elements as a
mimetic realism or vulgar sensation might demand. The
emotion is always fixed upon idea, not upon personality.*[51]

Noh theatre has been described by Western critics as
being barely recognisable as theatre at all: a stage
stripped bare as a boxing ring; no action but the
recollection of action; ambiguous story-telling; an
arbitrary and fragmented text; and a pace that slows
down time, altering the viewer's perceptions and
insistently focusing on the present. As Donald Richie
notes: 'There exists only the extraordinary bond
between the mind of the actor and the minds of the
audience. There is nothing else. It is pure and naked
theatre.'[52] This is theatre as an object of contemplation,
a stop that occurs somewhere along the line between

Conceptual art and contemporary notions of drama. The way in which a Noh actor prepares for the stage — sitting before a mirror, facing his own reflected image and putting on his mask — has been beautifully described by Kunio Komparu, a 22nd-generation Noh performer:

As he gazes intently through the tiny pupil eyeholes at the figure in the mirror, a kind of willpower is born, and the image — another self that is another — begins to approach the actor's everyday internal self and eventually the self and this other absorb one another to become a single existence transcending self and other. This too we might call magic by will power: the functions of mirror and mask merge as a spirit is incarnated and the self transformed by the magic of strengthened autosuggestion. When the time comes to go onstage, he fixes his mind on the stage as the mirror and himself as the image and then devotes himself completely to the magic of performance, which is meant to be shared with the audience and its group mind.[53]

'The mask inspires me,' Jonas has said about her own work and the masks she has used continually over the years — ranging from Mexican devils and painted dolls to a PVC hockey face guard, recalling the 1980 slasher movie *Friday the 13th*. 'If you put a mask on you can enter a different world.'[54] There's an unworn mask that is sometimes seen lying on the studio floor in *I Want to Live in the Country (And Other Romances)*; it's a prop that is never called into play, a latent piece of inspiration. For Jonas the mask provided a way to erase personal identity and the expectation of the autobiographical, and to achieve a new identity created solely for the public. In *I Want to Live in the Country (And Other Romances)*, we never see the face of the woman in white: her identity is erased by the careful framing and cropping of the screen image. This time, as the objects in the studio are reshuffled, the mask disappears.

In a documentary about director Yasujiro Ozu, the actor Chishyu Ryu recalled Ozu telling him to think of his face as a Noh mask and avoid any display of emotion.[55] Ozu, who claimed that he only went to see foreign films, praised Bette Davis's performance in *The Little Foxes*: playing a ruthless wife, she makes tea while her husband is dying; her face is impassive, mute as a mask; and the only sound is the click of the teacup against the saucer.[56] Here, the devastating presence of objects reveals an innate and disquieting poetry.

'Transition is one of the most difficult things — the in-between parts, getting from one section to the next in one work,' Jonas has said.[57] In Ozu's films, transitions occur remarkably: a cutaway from a scene with actors to an inanimate object, from human drama to a still life. 'Pillow shot' is the term that Noel Burch devised to describe this; it's an analogy to the pillow word used in Japanese poetry dating back to the ninth century, a decentering epithet that creates a separate space, taking the reader out of the poem, providing a reminder that man is not the centre of the universe. In the pillow shot, the camera cuts away to an inanimate object — a vase of flowers, a chimney, laundry on a clothesline. To move directly from one

thing to another, Jonas recognised, was an elegant
solution. As Tom Milne has pointed out about the deep
tranquility and reconciliation that pervades Ozu's
films: 'Each of his scenes is introduced by an object,
durable and immovable; against it, his characters
live out their lives, and long after their suffering
has ended, the object will endure.'[58]

In the blue screen studio, a globe of the world spins,
nearly filling the screen. 'I am lying in the field
trying to stay awake under the stars,' intones the
voiceover. 'Watching the trees for smoke, listening
for crackling, in case it happens again.' The camera
views alter and sometimes we catch glimpse of a hand.
The globe is hollow and the woman in white twirls
her finger in a hole at the top of world. 'Fire travels
underground by the roots,' the voiceover continues.
'You can't know where it will surface.' Once again,
the recollection of ordinary activities, untethered
and re-presented, conveys the power of myth.

'The women were all watching until the end,' says the
voiceover in another vignette. We see the studio blacked
out, but still framed in red. In place of the blue screen,
a black-and-white film plays within the frame: the
woman in white performs her solitary, disconcerting
dance. She swings her skirts and dashes about, sitting
down for a second, spinning around, and dashing off
again. Her full skirt cascades behind her and swishes
through the air as she turns. A piece of repetitive
country music plays in the background. The black-and-
white film rolls continuously, a horizontal roll like

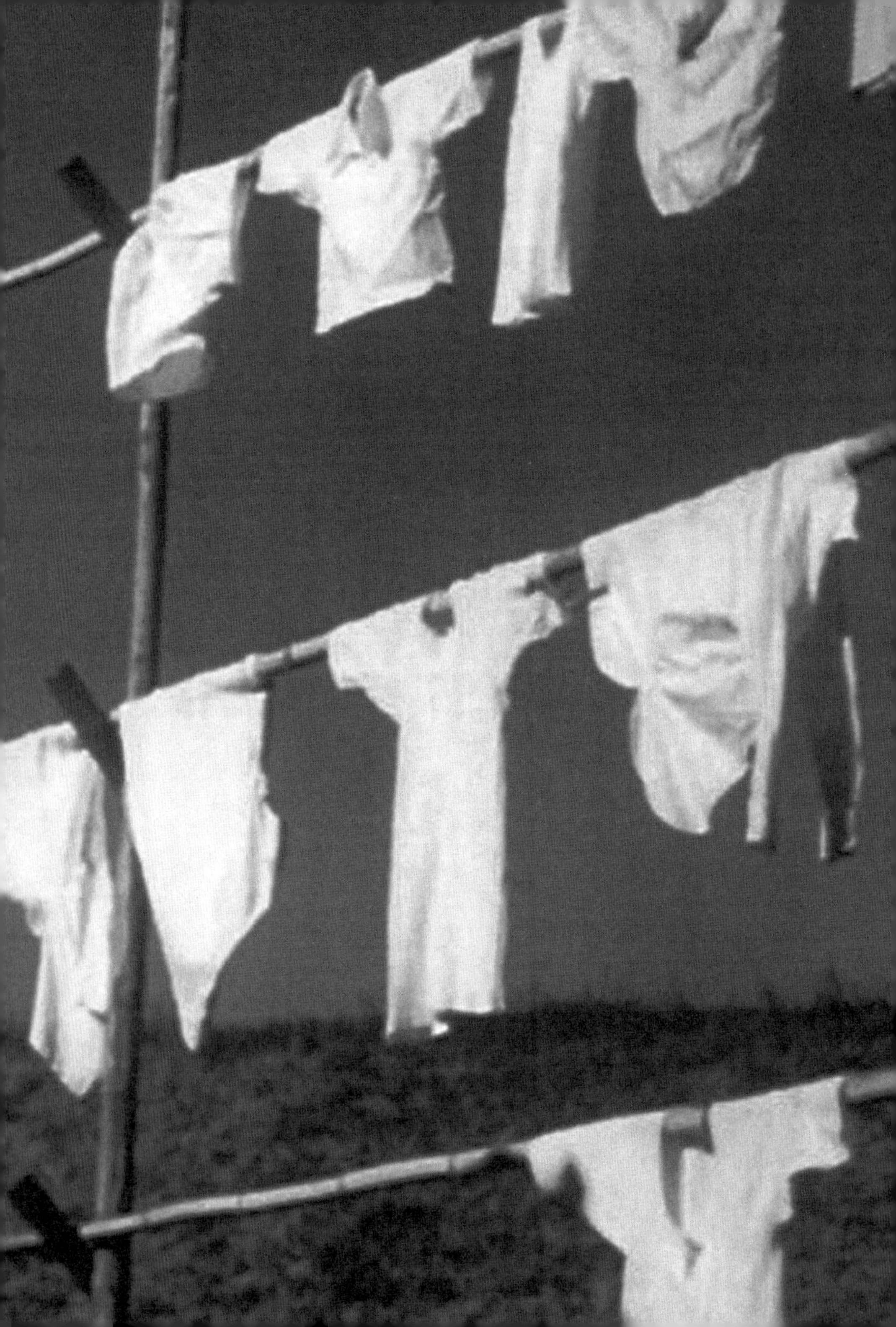

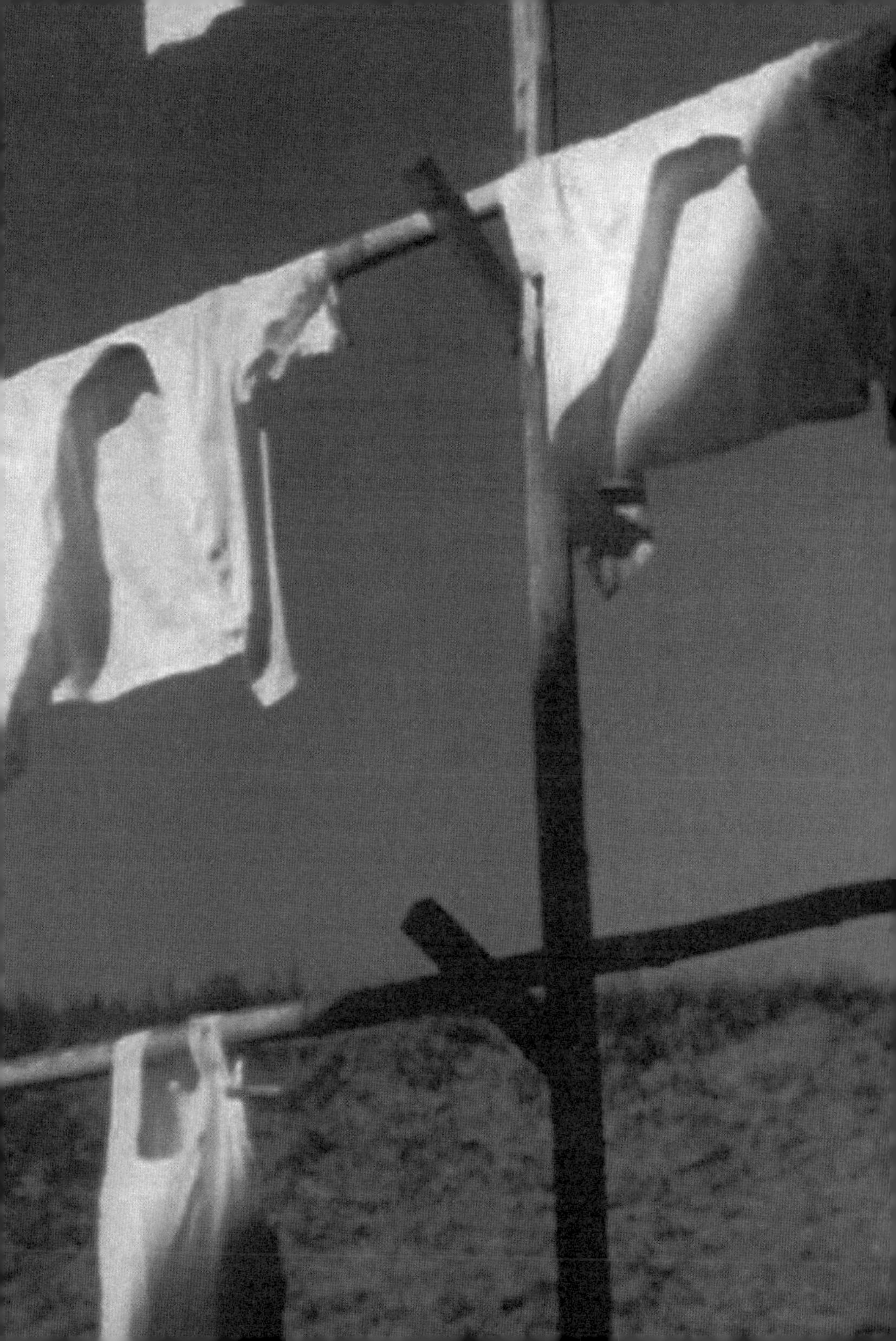

a zoetrope turning, or a joking reference to *Vertical Roll*. The voiceover continues: 'And then suddenly we were all running around the charred trees. Stamping on the coals.' The pronouns shift again and the nameless narrator escapes us.

Jonas's work is constructed intentionally from fragments — a partially played tune, a piece of conversation repeated, a fusion of images. In an interview published in one of her exhibition catalogues, the perplexed interlocutor asks: 'If the viewer is left to find the connections among all the elements presented in a piece, doesn't it mean that no two people see the performance in the same way?' The unperturbed artist answers, 'Of course.'[59] I think it was Merce Cunningham who, in response to a similarly fretful query, remarked that a collection of disparate elements presented together wasn't really any different than looking at page of newspaper stories. It's the basic theory of collage: two distinct realities are placed on a plane that is foreign to both of them. You put one thing next to another and it makes something else, a third thing, a visual poem.

'I am constructing the piece in relation to the set, to the moving frames, the frame of the video, the frame of the glass table, the space,' Jonas wrote in 1994, while preparing her multi-media performance work *Revolted by the thought of known places… Sweeney Astray.*[60] 'We move through fragmented time, step by step filmically constructing the sound, each scene, the breaks, the transitions, the light.'[61] Jonas's work comes together

in an amalgam of varied fragments: selected elements
and planned juxtapositions that are often catalysed
through improvisational techniques or chance
operations. As the narrator remarks in Donald
Barthelme's oft-quoted 1964 story 'See the Moon?':
'Fragments are the only form I trust.'[62]

Throughout *I Want to Live in the Country (And Other
Romances)* an old-timey piece of country music recurs,
in unfinished scraps, on the soundtrack. The tune
floats in and out, rises exuberantly, then, lowers
to a whisper, going silent. Although we never hear
the entire song, the melody feels achingly familiar.
Jonas uses 'popular song as a found object' — a phrase
that P. Adams Sitney coined to describe Kenneth Anger's
soundtracks.[63] In Anger's *Scorpio Rising* a Technicolour
Jesus and his Apostles take a Palm Sunday stroll to the
yearning up-tempo sound of Little Peggy March singing
'I Will Follow Him'. As an admirer of Anger's film
(first screened in New York by Jonas Mekas in 1966),
Jonas has always been delighted by that particular
sequence — its surprising wit and succinct beat.

The teasing bit of country music that recurs in *I Want
to Live in the Country (And Other Romances)* is first
heard at the end of an interior sequence — like a reel
calling out to the dancers. It's an instrumental refrain:
flat-picking guitar-playing that dips rhythmically
in a tune that goes round and round. Just before one
quick cut from the interior to the countryside, we hear
a few lines of the chorus as a male singer breaks into
a yodel:

When the roses come again
When the roses come again
I will meet you I will greet you
When the roses come again

It's a bluegrass song called 'When the Roses Come Again', recorded by the Carter Family in 1933, that catches — in its repetitions, circularity and plain-spoken language — the cyclical ways of love and nature.

Interior: the woman in white kneels by the blackboard, repeatedly drawing concentric arcs — gentle curves bending from the upper-left hand corner down to the lower right. 'A gesture has for me the same weight as a drawing,' wrote Jonas in a 1983 artist's statement. 'Draw, erase, draw, erase — memory erased.'[64] In Jonas's work, repetitive drawing is a basic element, making a mark, inscribing a memory. In 1976 at the Anthology Film Archives, she saw a four-hour version of *Divine Horsemen*, Maya Deren's unedited documentary footage of Haitian Vodoun rituals. In one scene, a man continuously makes a drawing in the sand, an action that Jonas found remarkably moving and disarmingly private.[65] Drawing, she has observed, is a visual language. Jonas found transcultural examples of endless drawing discussed in *Spiritual Disciplines* — a 1970 anthology of Eranos lectures on mythology, religion and psychology edited by Joseph Campbell — and was especially interested in anthropologist/Jungian analyst John Leyard's accounts of New Guinean maze dancing, labyrinths and sand tracing.[66] For Jonas, the experience of repetitive drawing is not solely an obsessive act; rather, it is something pleasurable, a living ritual caught up in rhythmic patterning and soothing recurrences.

I Want to Live in the Country (And Other Romances) occurs — like all of Jonas's work — slightly outside of any given era. As the woman in white draws concentric arcs on the blackboard and the silent woman remains fixed in the corner of the screen, the voiceover reads:

They calculated things by the shape of clouds, the length of shadows, and the flight of birds. By two flies on a flat rock. By throwing bones over their left shoulders and by every kind of trick and game.

The language and the woman, dressed in her plain shirtwaist, are curiously timeless. The woman in white's appearance hints at an archetypal American past, a daydream redolent of unembellished Shaker beauty, Emily Dickinson's signature white costume or the farmer's wife joyously leaping in Martha Graham's choreography for Aaron Copland's *Appalachian Spring* (1944). She is the only performer to appear in *I Want to Live in the Country (And Other Romances)*. There is no doubt that the room she inhabits is stifling.

Jonas shot two entirely separate bodies of work for *I Want to Live in the Country (And Other Romances)*: the scenes of the countryside and the studio interior. As Charles Ruas points out, the footage was edited and joined together in a way that is similar to an audio literary structure: a reading, a set piece (the interior) alternating with a literary conversation, a more spontaneous flow (the exterior), 'The text externalises an internal mood,' notes Ruas, 'but the images and text don't illustrate. They bounce off each other.'[67]

Interior: In the windowless studio, the woman in white races between a chair and a stool, swings around, starts to lose her balance, and swings again, changing direction. On the soundtrack, there is the sound of wind and sputter of spreading fire. 'Last night we turned on the TV for the first time in weeks. Poltergeist lifting and moving furniture,' intones the voiceover. 'A child thrown against the wall. The smell of sulphur.'

The narrative structure of *I Want to Live in the Country (And Other Romances)* is not linear. If there is a story, it is constructed through contrasts, the linking of *non sequiturs* and disjunctive images: the confined interior and the wide open spaces; the reverie of a summer's day and the demands of the studio; the ominous qualities of nature and the potency of dreams. Yvonne Rainer asked in 'A Likely Story', a paper she delivered for a panel at the 1976 Edinburgh Film Festival:

Can an audience learn to abandon its narrative expectation once that expectation has been aroused by narrative elements in the work? What kinds of clues tell us, the audience, when to read an image — or a series of images — narratively, when to read them parataxically and when to read them iconographically? What constitutes continuity in the movies and what kind of clue tells us to 'begin again?' Why this urgency in our acculturated and suppurating brain that

*propels us to find connections between what we simultane-
ously see and hear, between what we have just seen
and what we are about to see? What constitutes unity in
film? Can the narrative and the other-than-narrative exist
simultaneously in the same shot, creating a kind of strobe
effect with regard to meaning?*[68]

Jonas delivers that strobe effect in *I Want to Live in the
Country (And Other Romances)*.

'Cage liberated us all to take chance — and chances — to
connect things,' said Jonas in the conversation recorded
for the Queens Museum of Art catalogue. In the autumn
of 1960, John Cage asked Robert Dunn, his former
student in music composition at The New School
in New York, to teach a composition class for dancers
at Merce Cunningham's studio. Dunn's teaching
was focused variously to incorporate ideas about Zen
Buddhism, philosophy, the nature of materials, new
music and ways to extend perceptive boundaries and
contexts. 'I had the notion in teaching of making a
"clearing",' wrote Dunn. 'A sort of "space of nothing"
in which things could appear and grow in their own
nature.'[69] Among Dunn's students were Rainer, Trisha
Brown, Simone Forti and Deborah Hay. Started in 1962,
the Judson Dance Theatre (and what became known
as postmodern dance) grew directly out of these classes.
In Dunn's class, they might be told to: 'Make a five-
minute dance in half an hour', 'Watch the dance you are
watching' or 'Take something, cut it up and reassemble
it'. Trisha Brown has described Dunn's workshop as
'the recombination of form and content'. A performance

might be someone eating a sandwich or overwhelmed by a crying jag, timed with a stopwatch.[70] In the lineage of influences, Jonas found a great deal of freedom in the workshops that she took with her contemporaries Hay, Brown and Rainer, who brought exalted dance down to human scale, investigating everyday movement and experience, creating a quotidian choreography.

In California, Brown, Forti and Rainer had all studied with Anna Halprin. Her techniques — improvisation, chance procedures, movement generated by everyday tasks, use of the voice while moving — had taken hold in their process. In the 1950s, Halprin had a realization as to how to approach dance and performance. 'One day as I was sitting for a long time outdoors on our wooded dance deck, I became aware of light on a tree, a red berry that fell at my side, a fog horn in the distance and children shouting; and I wondered if they were really in trouble or just playing. These chance relationships, each independent of the other, seemed beautiful to me.'[71]

Borges wrote that dreaming and wakefulness are the pages of a single book and that to read them in order is to live, and to leaf through them at random, to dream.[72] In *I Want to Live in the Country (And Other Romances)* the elements of chance and the careful distilling of information unfold like the pages of a single book, gently balanced between wakefulness and dreaming.

Exterior: 'You see something in the distance,' says the voiceover, as the Super 8 camera picks out the landscape, moving furtively in curious glances, darting about — up and down, right and left. The open fields are sunburnt yellow and green. In the foreground, tall grasses stir in the wind and the filmed space appears deeper, the immeasurable expanse more defined: the wide field, the distant house, the wider ocean. The voiceover continues: 'Then, when you get there and look back, things seem so different from what you imagined.'

p.10
Giorgio De Chirico
Canzone d'amore (Love Song),
oil on canvas, 73x59.1cm, 1914
The Museum of Modern Art, New York
Copyright: DACS, London 2006

p.15
Joan Jonas, *Organic Honey's Vertical Roll*,
performance, Musée Galleria, Paris, 1972
Photograph: Beatrice Helligers

pp.60—61
Joan Jonas, *Lines in the Sand*,
performance, Documenta 11,
(performers: Ragani Haas, Henk Visch,
Sung Hwan Kim; sound/music:
Paul Miller aka DJ Spooky), 2002
Photograph: Werner Maschmann

pp.66—67
Robert Frank, *Words, Nova Scotia*,
gelatin silver print, 40.5x50.5cm, 1977
Copyright: National Gallery of Canada, Ottawa

pp.70—71
Joan Jonas, *Mirror Piece 1*, Performance,
Leob Student Center, NYU, 1969
Photograph: Wayne Hollingworth

pp.76—77
Federico Fellini, *The Nights of Cabiria*,
1957, 117min

pp.84—85
Yasujiro Ozu, *Tokyo Story*, 1953, 136min

1
Francesco Petrarca, *De Vita Solitaria*, 1356, quoted in frontispiece of Helen
and Scott Nearing's *Living the Good Life*, New York: Schoken Books, 1970.

2
Valerie Smith and Warren Niesluchowski (eds.), *Joan Jonas: Five Works*,
New York: Queens Museum of Art, 2003, p.128.

3
Joan Simon, 'Scenes and Variations: An Interview with Joan Jonas',
Art in America, July 1995, p.76.

4
The accelerated history of the early days of video art has been recorded
in a great variety of accounts ranging from the anecdotal to the academic.
An essential contemporaneous anthology produced by artists is Ira Schneider
and Beryl Korot (eds.), *Video Art*, New York: Harcourt Brace Jovanovich,
1976. John Hanhardt, currently senior curator of Film and Media Arts
at the Guggenheim Museum in New York, has written extensively about
video; he was the editor of *Video Culture: A Critical Investigation*, Salt Lake
City, Utah: Gibbs M. Smith Inc./Peregrine Books, 1986. Hanhardt's anthology
includes essays by Louis Althusser, Walter Benjamin, Douglas Crimp,
Rosalind Krauss and David Ross.

Electronic Arts Intermix, founded by the innovative art dealer Howard Wise
in 1971, continues to be the outstanding source and resource for video artists.
In New York in May 1969, Wise presented the landmark video exhibition 'TV
as a Creative Medium'. Among the many services and primary information
offered by Electronic Arts Intermix is their website and its extensive
archive: http://www.eai.org

Chris Hill, a video curator and independent scholar, helped compile the
17-hour programme *Surveying the First Decade: Video Art and Alternative
Media* in the U.S. for the Video Data Bank; founded in Chicago in 1976,
the Video Data Bank (http://www.vdb.org) is one of the leading resources
in the United States for videotapes by and about contemporary artists.
Hill's comprehensive 1995 video history *Attention! Production! Audience!:
Performing Video in the in the First Decade, 1968–1980* is available online at
http://www.experimentaltvcenter.org, a site which hosts the Video History
Project, a volunteer-run resource for texts, biographies and interviews.

Information about an in-progress documentary film, *TV Lab 1972–1984:
Funding Creativity*, produced and directed by Howard Weinberg, is available
at http://www.howardweinberg.net. Initial funders for this documentary
included Nam June Paik and the Rockefeller Foundation.

Clearly, as more publications and institutions continue to consider this era,
the literature will grow. *Artforum* writer and editor Eric C. Banks wrote in

the magazine's September 2001 issue (archived at http://www.artforum.com)
'The opening years of the 1970s heralded a revolution when it came to
artists' investment in the "temporal art" — or so the conventional wisdom
would have it. The revolution came in the form of Sony's lightweight,
low-cost Portapak video camera; historical ground zero was Nam June
Paik's 1965 purchase of one of the earliest prototypes available to the public.
The aftershocks, which rippled through SoHo as wave after wave of artists
armed themselves with the easy to use, bargain basement camera, are still
being felt today.'

5
For additional accounts of the TV Lab and WNET/Channel 13,
see http://www.thirteen.org/reelnewyork2/overview.html and
http://www.experimentaltvcenter.org

6
A.P. [sic], 'Special Effects Pioneer Arthur Widmer Dies', *Hollywood Reporter*,
5 June 2006.

7
In the Video Data bank catalogue (http://www.vdb.org), the description
of *I Want To Live in the Country (And Other Romances)* reads: 'Jonas intercuts
scenes of the Nova Scotia countryside with images of a studio set-up
reminiscent of a de Chirico painting.' The summary of *I Want To Live
in the Country (And Other Romances)* featured in Douglas Crimp (ed.), *Joan
Jonas, Scripts and Descriptions*, Berkeley, California: University Art Museum,
University of California, 1983, p.134, also mentions de Chirico: 'Jonas uses
the artificial studio situation set-up with still lifes reminiscent of de
Chirico using such props as a bronze horse, a globe, a tin cone, a paper cone
and a blackboard.'

8
V. Smith and W. Niesluchowski, *Joan Jonas: Five Works*, *op. cit.*, p.136.

9
Joan Jonas, *Joan Jonas*, Southampton: John Hansard Gallery, 2004, p.11.

10
Letter to the author, 28 May 2006.

11
Diana Rico, *Kovacsland*, New York and London: Harcourt Brace Jovanovich,
1990, pp.202—04.

12
Conversation with the author, 18 April 2006, Los Angeles.

13

V. Smith and W. Niesluchowski, *Joan Jonas: Five Works*, *op. cit.*, p.135.

14

I. Schneider and B. Korot (eds.), *Video Art*, *op. cit.*, p.73.

15

The works of Portuguese writer Fernando Antonio Nogueira Pessoa
(1888—1935) were all written by his alter egos — various characters
with complex individual biographies, distinct influences and literary
styles. Referring to these identities as 'heteronyms', Pessoa has said
they were created to 'other himself'. Writing about Pessoa in *The Observer*
(3 June 2001), George Steiner remarked: 'The fragmentary, the incomplete,
is the essence of Pessoa's spirit. The very kaleidoscope of voices with
him, the breadth of his culture, the catholicity of his ironic sympathies
— wonderfully echoed in Saramago's great novel about Ricardo Reis
— inhibited the monumentalities, the self-satisfaction of completion.'
Reis and Saramago were both heteronyms of Pessoa's: one invented
character wrote about another's invented life. Describing *The Book of
Disquiet* (Penguin Classics, 2002), his major prose work, Pessoa himself
said, 'It's all fragments, fragments, fragments.'

16
I. Schneider and B. Korot, *Video Art*, *op. cit.* p.73

17
Quoted in the biographical entry for Samuel (Barclay) Beckett in
Encyclopaedia Britannica, Micropaedia Vol. 2, Chicago: Encyclopaedia
Britannica, Inc., 1978, p.33.

18
V. Smith and W. Niesluchowski, *Joan Jonas: Five Works*, *op. cit.*, p.127.

19
In a conversation that appears in V. Smith and W. Niesluchowski, *Joan
Jonas: Five Works*, *op. cit.*, p.129, Jonas observes, 'Going to Japan in 1970 was
another transforming experience. It was the first time I had been to the
East, and I went during a period when I was trying to find an alternative
language, one beyond Minimalism. Noh is a visual dance theatre, closer
to what I was interested in and something I could identify with. It's
more abstract, and I learned afterwards that is also what attracted Antonin
Artaud to Eastern theatre. It's not entirely based on text. Since I didn't
understand the language, I wasn't following the text. Its poetic aspect is
what interested W.B. Yeats and Ernest Fenollosa.' Serra accompanied Jonas,
and in a 1978 interview with Liza Bear (originally printed in *Avalanche*,
30 March 1978, n.p.), he referred to the importance of the trip, which
coincided with the Tokyo Biennale : 'There was a convergence of events
that made me rethink scale. I had completed a series of large scale stacking

pieces at Kaiser Steel; I helped Bob Smithson stake out *Spiral Jetty* and later I visited the Zen Gardens of Kyoto, Mio Sinji, Ryoan-Ji, Tokai-An, and upon my return I visited Heizer's piece (*Double Negative*).' Bear's piece is reprinted in Richard Serra and Clara Weyergraf, *Richard Serra: Interviews, Etc. 1970–1980*, Yonkers: The Hudson River Museum, 1980, p.70.

20
J. Simon, 'Scenes and Variations: An Interview with Joan Jonas', *op. cit.*, p. 76

21
D. Crimp (ed.), *Joan Jonas, Scripts and Descriptions, op. cit.*, n.p.

22
Conversation with the author, 6 April 1996.

23
Dorrine Mignot (ed.), *Joan Jonas: Works 1968–1994*, Amsterdam: Stedelijk Museum, 1994, p.33.

24
Ray L. Birdwhistell, *Kinesics and Context: Essays on Body Motion Communication*, Philadelphia : University of Pennsylvania Press, 1970. Birdwhistell (1918–1994), American anthropologist and former dancer, was an expert on nonverbal communication and expression through gesture and posture. With J.D. Van Vlack, he made a series of films based on his lectures observing human dynamics and interactions. Perhaps the best known film in the series, produced by the Eastern Pennsylvania Psychiatric Institute, is *Microcultural Incidents at Ten Zoos*, in which Birdwhistell and Van Vlack focused on the interactions of human families and animals in zoos in England, France, Italy, Hong Kong, India, Japan and the United States.

25
Annette Michelson, 'The Films of Richard Serra', *October*, no.10, Fall 1979, p.81.

26
P. Adams Sitney, *Visionary Film: The American Avant Garde, 1943–1978*, Oxford and New York: Oxford University Press, 1979, p.125.

27
Sergei M. Eisenstein, *Immoral Memories: An Autobiography*, trans. Herbert Marshall, Boston: Houghton Mifflin Company, 1983, p.76.

28
V. Smith and W. Niesluchowski, *Joan Jonas: Five Works, op. cit*, p.133.

29
For more about Jack Smith, see Edward Leffingwell, Carole Kismaric
and Marvin Heiferman (eds.), *Jack Smith: Flaming Creature, His Amazing
Life and Times*, London and New York: The Institute of Contemporary Art
and P.S.1/Serpent's Tail, 1997; and *Jack Smith and the Destruction of Atlantis*,
a 2006 documentary film about the artist, produced and directed by Mary
Jordan (http://www.jacksmithandthedestructionofatlantis.com).

30
Letter to the author, *op. cit.*

31
Lynn Keller, 'An Interview with Susan Howe', *Contemporary Literature*,
Vol. 36 no. 1, Spring 1995, n.p. Archived online at:
http://muse.jhu.edu/journals/contemporary_literature

32
Ruas was also a friend and editor of the incomparable American writer
Marguerite Young (1908—1995). At WBAI, he and Wynne produced an audio
performance of her picaresque, hallucinatory epic novel *Miss MacIntosh, My
Darling*. When the documentary filmmaker D.A. Pennebaker was asked, in an
interview for *Sight and Sound*, to select his favourite soundtrack, he named
this radio production — with a soundtrack imaginatively conjured up from
humming goblets and shattered glass to an 'incredible' and 'haunting' effect.

33
J. Simon, 'Scenes and Variations: An Interview with Joan Jonas', *op. cit.*, p.76

34
Philip Glass, *Music by Philip Glass*, Robert T. Jones (ed.), New York: Harper &
Row Publishers, 1987, p.8.

35
H. and S. Nearing, *Living the Good Life*, *op. cit.*, p.ix.

36
Robert Frank, *Robert Frank*, New York: Aperture, 1976, np.

37
Anne Wilkes Tucker and Philip Brookman (eds.), *Robert Frank: New York
to Nova Scotia*, Boston: Little Brown and Company, 1986, p.62.

38
Conversation with the author, *op. cit.*, 18 April 2006.

39
A. W. Tucker and P. Brookman (eds.), *Robert Frank: New York to Nova Scotia*,
op. cit., p.88.

40
Conversation with the author, *op. cit.*

41
V. Smith and W. Niesluchowski, *Joan Jonas: Five Works*, *op. cit.*, p.127.

42
J. Simon, 'Scenes and Variations: An Interview With Joan Jonas', *op. cit.*, p.76.

43
Letter to the author, *op. cit.*

44
Richard Burgin, *Conversations with Jorge Luis Borges*, New York, Chicago, San Francisco: Holt, Rhinehart and Winston, 1968, p.16.

45
Jorge Luis Borges, *Borges: Selected Non-Fictions*, Eliot Weinberger (ed.), trans. Esther Allen and Suzanne Jill Levine, New York: Penguin Group, New York, 1999, p.160.

46
V. Smith and W. Niesluchowski, *Joan Jonas: Five Works*, *op. cit.*, p.94.

47
Ibid. p.133.

48
H.D. (Hilda Doolittle), *Collected Poems, 1912–1944*, Louis L. Martz (ed.), New York: New Directions, 1983, p.15.

49
V. Smith and W. Niesluchowski, *Joan Jonas: Five Works*, *op. cit.*, p.8.

50
Donald Richie, *A Lateral View: Essays on Culture and Style in Contemporary Japan*, Berkeley: Stone Bridge Press, 1992, p.113.

51
Ernest Fenollosa and Ezra Pound, *The Classic Noh Theatre of Japan*, New York: New Directions, 1959, p.69.

52
D. Richie, *A Lateral View: Essays on Culture and Style in Contemporary Japan*, *op. cit.*, p.124.

53
Kunio Komparu, *The Noh Theatre: Principles and Perspectives*, New York: John Weatherwill Publishers Inc., 1984, p.8.

54
V. Smith and W. Niesluchowski, *Joan Jonas: Five Works*, *op. cit*, p.129.

55
Kazuo Inoue, 'I Lived, But...', documentary film, 1963; included in *Tokyo Story*, special edition, Criterion Collection DVD, 1983.

56
David Bordwell, *Ozu and the Poetics of Cinema*, Princeton: Princeton University Press, 1988, p.85.

57
V. Smith and W. Niesluchowski, *Joan Jonas: Five Works*, *op. cit*, p.131.

58
Tom Milne, *Sight and Sound: A Fiftieth Anniversary Selection*, David Wilson (ed.), London: Faber and Faber Ltd. with B.F.I., 1982, p.176.

59
Joan Jonas, *Joan Jonas*, *op. cit.*, p.11.

60
Produced in conjunction with 'Joan Jonas: Works 1968—1994', Stedelijik Museum, Amsterdam; Co-production: Toneelgroep Amsterdam and Stedelijik Museum in association with Holland Festival. Based on *Sweeney Astray* by Seamus Heaney, Dutch translation by Jan Eijkelboom.

61
D. Mignot, *Joan Jonas: Works 1968–1994*, *op. cit.*, p.89.

62
Donald Barthelme, *Sixty Stories*, New York: G.P. Putnam's Sons, 1981, p.98. Mel Bochner, in 'Secrets of the Domes', an *Artforum* (September 2006, p.345) piece about his 1966 collaboration with Robert Smithson, *The Domain of The Great Bear* (a magazine project for *Art Voices*, Fall 1966), writes: 'Donald Barthelme, one of the great progenitors of postmodern fiction, told us one night at Max's Kansas City how "The Domain of the Great Bear" had influenced his own writing when he first read it. He commissioned Bob and me to write something about "humour in art" for an issue of a new fiction magazine he was editing. We were excited by the prospect of working together again, and although the project would be cut short by Bob's tragic accident, we immediately began some preliminary readings on the subject: Baudelaire, Freud and Marx (Groucho, not Karl).'

63
P. Adams Sitney, *Visionary Film: The American Avant Garde*, *op. cit.*, p.118—22.

64
D. Crimp, *Joan Jonas, Scripts and Descriptions*, *op. cit.*, p.137.

65
V. Smith and W. Niesluchowski, *Joan Jonas: Five Works*, *op. cit.*, p.130.

66
D. Crimp, *Joan Jonas, Scripts and Descriptions*, *op. cit.*, p.138. Jonas refers to
a collection of essays edited by Joseph Campbell, *Spiritual Disciplines: Papers
from the Eranos Yearbooks*, trans. Ralph Manheim, Princeton: Princeton
Univeristy Press, 1970.

67
Conversation with the author, 29 May 2006.

68
Yvonne Rainer, *A Woman Who...: Essays, Interviews, Scripts*, Baltimore
and London: The Johns Hopkins University Press, 1999, p.139—40.

69
Sally Banes, *Democracy's Body: Judson Dance Theatre, 1962—64*, Ann Arbor:
UMI Research Press, 1983, p.5.

70
Anne Livet (ed.), *Contemporary Dance*, New York: Abbeville Press, 1978, p.45.

71
Anna Halprin, as quoted by Richard Kostelanetz (ed.), in *Merce Cunningham:
Dancing in Space and Time*, Chicago: Chicago Review Press, Inc., 1992, p. xiii.

72
J.L. Borges, *Borges: Selected Non-Fictions*, *op. cit.*, p.162.